The Life and Times of
THE
MARX
BROTHERS

The Life and Times of
THE
MARX
BROTHERS

Ronald Bergan

SMITHMARK

This edition first published in 1992 by SMITHMARK Publishers Inc.,
112 Madison Avenue, New York, NY 10016

ISBN 0–8317–5806–6

Consultant editor: Robyn Karney

Design by Millions Design, London

Typeset by Cambrian Typesetters, Frimley, Surrey

Printed and bound in Hong Kong

SMITHMARK books are available for bulk purchases for sales promotion and
premium use. For details write or telephone the Manager of Special Sales,
SMITHMARK Publishers Inc., 112 Madison Avenue, New York, NY 10016.
(212) 532–6600.

Picture Credits and Acknowledgements

The publisher would like to thank the following:

Jane Burns and the Stills Department at the BFI

Gilbert Gibson
Aquarius Picture Library
(6, 8, 12, 17, 25, 27, 30, 33, 39, 42–3, 52–3, 56, 67, 76, 77, 78,
79, 94–5, 105, 121, 122, 123, 124, 125)

Joel Finler Collection
(68–9, 88–9, 91, 93, 98–9, 106, 112, 119)

Popperfoto
(13 [3 pictures], 14–15, 67 [2 pictures], 73, 114, 124 [2 pictures])

The Hulton-Deutsch Collection
(13)

CONTENTS

'WHATEVER IT IS, I'M AGAINST IT'

The Marx Brothers ran through Hollywood movies of the thirties and forties like naughty children let loose in a toy shop, causing hilarious chaos wherever they went – on board ship, in a college, at the opera, in Casablanca . . .

Once upon a mad time, there were five of them who, under the guidance of their formidable mother, Minnie Marx, built up a highly individual comic vaudeville act. They were, in descending order or age, Leonard, Adolph, Julius, Milton and Herbert, better known as Chico, Harpo, Groucho, Gummo and Zeppo.

After three smash Broadway musicals, the brothers (without Gummo, who hated performing), burst onto the screen in *The Cocoanuts* in 1929, immediately establishing the zany humour that made them into the movies' most anarchic and funniest comedy team. The Marx Brothers went on to make four more films for Paramount, before Irving Thalberg at MGM signed three of the Marxes up. (The good-looking Zeppo, the ineffectual romantic straight man, left to become an agent). They continued to run riot through a further eight movies before finally splitting up as a team in 1949.

Echoing Groucho's anti-conformist song in *Horse Feathers*, 'Whatever It Is I'm Against It', they were at their best when puncturing pomposity and throwing logic to the winds.

'People all have inhibitions and hate them,' explained Harpo. 'We just ignore them. Every man wants to chase a pretty girl if he sees one. He doesn't – I do. We're sort of a safety valve through which people can blow off steam.'

Groucho, with a large, black, painted-on moustache and eyebrows, rimless spectacles, long cigar, ill-fitting suit and crouched walk, was the master of the wisecrack and the put-down, and had a way of looking at women that made him known as 'King Leer'. His running courtship of the mountainous but rich Margaret Dumont, alternating between love talk and insults, is one of the great delights of the seven films they made together.

> **Groucho:** We were young, gay, reckless. That night I drank champagne from your slipper. Two quarts. It would have been more, but you were wearing inner soles . . . I could dance with you till the cows come home. On second thought I'd rather dance with the cows till you come home . . . Would you mind giving me a lock of your hair?
>
> **Dumont:** A lock of my hair? Why, I had no idea.
>
> **Groucho:** I'm letting you off easy. I was going to ask you for the whole wig.

LEFT
A poster for the first Marx Brothers film, The Cocoanuts *(1929), which immediately established their screen fame after they had successfully run riot on stage.*

ABOVE
'A lock of my hair? Why I had no idea.' The wonderful Junoesque Margaret Dumont being courted the first of many times on screen by Groucho in The Cocoanuts.

Chico, in a motley assortment of clothes and a leprechaun's hat above a mop of black hair, had a mischievous grin and enjoyed punning excrutiatingly in his exaggerated Italian accent. His eccentric, often one-fingered, piano playing was always a moment to cherish.

> Groucho:
>   (to Chico at the piano)
>   How much do you get an hour to play?
>   Chico: Six-a dollars, boss.
>   Groucho: How much would you take not to play?
>   Chico: Oh, you-a couldn't afford it.

Then there was a wordless Harpo, who continued the art of silent comedy into the talkies. In his woolly wig, loose-fitting coat with cavernous pockets from which he extracted everything including the kitchen sink – in *Horse Feathers*, he responds to a down-and-out's plea to help him get a cup of coffee, by producing a steaming hot cup of coffee from an inside pocket – wielding a pair of enormous scissors destructively, tooting his taxi horn while chasing blondes, hanging his leg over people's arms, and playing the harp like a fallen angel.

In real life, the thrice-married Groucho was crotchety, careful with his money, intellectual and extremely witty; Harpo was lovable, quiet and domesticated; Chico was ruled by two passions all his life – gambling and women, in that order – and was always broke.

Once he wrote a cheque out to pay a gambling debt, but asked the man not to cash it before twelve noon the next day if he wanted it to go through. The man waited, cashed it, and it still bounced. When he reproached Chico, Chico asked 'What time did you cash it?' 'Five minutes past twelve,' said the man. 'Too late,' replied Chico.

The brothers were, and still are, the darlings of both the general public and the intellectuals who saw them as true descendants of the surrealist movement. People as diverse as Winston Churchill, George Bernard Shaw and T. S. Eliot were fans. Some of Groucho's sayings have entered the language, such as his remark in a letter explaining why he was resigning from the Hillcrest Country Club: 'I don't want to belong to any club that would have me as a member.' (This was the inspiration behind the founding of the Groucho Club in London.) As the American essayist and broadcaster Clifton Fadiman wrote, 'The Marxes were so confidently unreasonable as to awaken in the spectator bitter doubts as to the worthwhileness of not being a fool.'

LEFT
The large, black, painted-on moustache and eyebrows, rimless spectacles and long cigar made Groucho instantly recognisable internationally. It was probably his bare-faced cheek to all and sundry, especially to pompous people, that gained him a following.

The Marx Brothers had ostensibly the most unlikely fans (anti-clockwise): the American Anglophile poet T.S. Eliot, cigar-smoking (like Groucho) Winston Churchill, Irish playwright George Bernard Shaw and Algonquin wit and humourist Dorothy Parker.

MINNIE'S BOYS

2

On the death of Minnie Marx on 28 September, 1929, *The New Yorker* wrote, 'She had done much more than bear her sons, bring them up, and turn them into play actors. She had invented them. They were just comics she imagined for her own amusement. They amused no one more, and their reward was her ravishing smile.' It was Minnie who conceived her sons' careers, shaped their early performances, and manoeuvred with all her tenacious skills to get them bookings. Harpo, writing of his mother in *Harpo Speaks*! says, 'She was a lovely woman, but her soft, doelike looks were deceiving. She had the stamina of a brewery horse, the drive of a salmon fighting his way up a waterfall, the cunning of a fox, and a devotion to her brood as fierce as any she-lion's.'

Minnie was fifteen by the time her parents came to the USA, and she went to work in a factory making straw hats. The family's relationship with show business dated back to her parents, Lafe and Fanny Schoenberg, who were performers in Germany before coming to America. Lafe worked as a magician and ventriloquist and Fanny was a yodelling harpist. But they found theatre work difficult to come by in the New World, so Lafe got a job fixing umbrellas. According to Groucho, 'It must have been the driest season in the New York weather bureau,' judging from the number of umbrellas he repaired. Fanny died shortly after the family moved to 179 East 93rd Street, which was to be the Marx home for many years. Lafe lived to be one hundred and one, despite smoking ten cigars a day made from leaves rejected from the tobacco factory.

Minnie was eighteen when she met Sam Marx at the dance school where he was an instructor, and they married soon after. He was from Alsace and had emigrated at seventeen to avoid being drafted. Because of his origins he was nicknamed Frenchie, and was known as such all his life. Shortly after the marriage, Sam set up in business as a tailor. It seems he was not very good at it, and he had a struggle to bring up his large family of five boys all housed in the East Side tenement. They arrived in the following order: Leonard (Chico) on March 22, 1887; Adolph (Harpo) on November 23, 1888; Julius (Groucho) on October 2, 1890, with Milton (Gummo) and Herbert (Zeppo) arriving in 1897 and 1901 respectively.

It was Minnie who first envisaged her sons as musical stage performers. Chico learnt to play the piano at twenty-five cents a lesson. As even that amount of money was a sacrifice, Chico was supposed to repeat every lesson he took for Harpo, but he was too busy

OVERLEAF
(From left to right) Harpo, Gummo, Chico and Groucho in 1916 already seasoned performers. Gummo left the troupe when he joined up during the First World War, and never performed again. He was replaced by Zeppo.

RIGHT
(From top to bottom) Groucho, Harpo, Gummo and Lon Levy during their early days in vaudeville. (Far right) The remarkable Minnie Marx, uncannily resembling Harpo, and (inset) her husband Sam, known to all as Frenchie.

16

BELOW
Harpo and the instrument with which he was synonymous. He had learnt to play as a child on his grandmother's old harp. Fanny Schoenberg had been a yodelling harpist in the Old world.

RIGHT
Groucho (left), at the age of twelve, considered the intellectual of the family. He had wanted to become a doctor. Harpo (with dog) was already, at fourteen, the quietest of the brothers.

with other activities, so Harpo had to struggle to learn the piano himself. Chico's teacher only knew how to play with his right hand and faked the left; that's why Chico became the best one-handed piano player in the neighborhood. Although Harpo did learn to play the piano well, it was his grandmother's old harp that really fascinated him. Groucho's musical talents lay in guitar-playing and singing. As a child, he would often sing to the accompaniment of Frenchie on the mandolin, Gummo and Minnie on guitars and Chico on the piano.

On Sundays he would sing soprano in a choir at an Episcopal church on Madison Avenue. Zeppo, too, had a good singing voice.

But the comic characters they later developed can be traced directly to their personalities as children. Because the family were always just one step ahead of economic disaster, Chico learnt to wheel and deal from an early age. He was always hustling money in one way or another around the bars, pool halls and race tracks that

he frequented. When something was missing from the apartment, it was pretty certain that Chico had pawned it, generally to get him enough money to buy into a poker game. After he graduated from the sixth grade he had a short-lived job in a lace shop, but never got his pay cheque home without betting it on something on the way. Gambling was the main passion and compulsion of his life; the rest of his family were always attempting to keep him from gambling his money away, often having to bail him out of trouble at the same time. 'There are three things that my brother Chico is always on,' Groucho once remarked. 'A phone, a horse, or a broad.'

Harpo was much quieter and more contemplative. At school the other kids used to tease and bully him, and one boy liked to drop Harpo out of the school's first floor window, an eight-foot fall. Dropped once too often, he decided never to return after the second grade. But he learned as quickly as Chico to survive by his wits. He would pick up items to sell to junk dealers, hang around tennis courts in the hope of getting a stray ball, and avoid the conductor on trolley cars. He also had a number of jobs; he worked as a pie sorter and as a butcher's delivery boy, but was fired for eating a customer's order of frankfurters. He was a bellhop at the Hotel Seville on 28th Street; walked the dog of a theatrical star; set pins in a bowling alley; worked in the garment district and in a shipping brokerage.

Harpo and Chico began buying miniature cuckoo clocks on the cheap and selling them for profit. Anxious to make a sale, Harpo told one potential customer that the clocks would only require winding every eight hours. While he kept the man talking, Harpo would give the chains of the clocks a pull.

In the window of a cigar store, in the back room of which Chico and some card sharks set up games, a man known as Gookie would wrap cigarettes, pulling the most awful faces at the same time. Harpo would stand and watch him for ages and then would amuse his friends by imitating the man's puffed up cheeks and cross-eyes, something he did in every Marx Brothers movie. Harpo also got laughs by wearing a blond wig he borrowed from Groucho while he was a delivery boy for a wig company.

LEFT
Chico trying to have his way with Ilona Massey in Love Happy (1949). Off-screen, the oldest Marx brother had a reputation as a skirt-chaser, hence the derivation of his nickname Chicko, soon changed to Chico. Yet women took second place to his other passion – gambling.

RIGHT
Harpo demonstrating, in A Day at the Races (1937), the grotesque look he would put on in every Marx Brothers movie, something he picked up as a kid while watching a man wrap cigarettes in a cigar store window. Much of his screen persona was formed early in life.

Groucho had wanted to become a doctor, but because his schooling had ended at thirteen the medical profession was deprived of his contribution to it. He enjoyed reading, and had a reputation as the intellectual of the family but, like his elder brothers, he was no mean operator. For example, Minnie would give him five pennies to go and buy a loaf of bread. He would buy a day-old loaf for four, keep the extra money and pass the bread off on his family as fresh.

Groucho got his reputation for being careful with money from the time he was around twelve. The story goes that he had saved exactly enough money to take a girl he fancied to Hammerstein's Victoria Theatre for a vaudeville show, but had failed to calculate for the five cents for the candy she wanted. Consequently, he had only one nickel left for the streetcar home and tossed her for it. He won, she walked.

After Groucho left school, he took a job as an office boy at $3.50 per week. his task was to answer phones, but as the boss was absent a great deal from the office, so was Groucho. One day, he was out and picked up a hat that had blown away. He returned it to the owner who happened to be his boss. Groucho then applied for a job as a boy singer with a small-time vaudeville act called the Le May Trio for four dollars a week plus room and board. But Le May disappeared with all the salary money, leaving Groucho stranded without a penny in Cripple Creek, Colorado. He had to sell his costume to pay the rent, so he took a job driving a horse and wagon. Back in New York, his mother helped him into another tour as a boy singer to an English actress. The actress ran away with the lion tamer and Groucho's money.

Meanwhile, Harpo was hired to play the piano in a brothel in Freeport, Long Island, after Chico had been sacked for being over-friendly with the girls. The madame was later arrested on charges of using the house as a receiving depot for stolen property.

It was time for Minnie to step in and organise her sons' careers. She was already acting as agent for her

Groucho demonstrating his intellectual curiosity in a scene from **Horse Feathers** *(1932), in which he played the crackpot president of a college.*

Groucho with his uncle Al Shean, Minnie's younger brother, who wrote material for the Marx Brothers early shows, and became well-known as *half of the popular comedy-singing double act of Gallagher and Shean. They appeared in a number of movie musicals in the 1930s.*

LEFT
Minnie surrounded by her devoted brood whom 'she had invented'. They are Zeppo (kneeling), Chico, Groucho and Harpo. Gummo had long since retired.

younger brother, Al, who had worked as a pants presser, but whose hobby was singing. She got him into vaudeville, and he eventually rose to the top when he changed his name from Shoenberg to Shean and teamed up with Ed Gallagher to become the popular comedy-singing act Gallagher and Shean. (Uncle Al recreated the act, with Charles Winninger, in the 1941 MGM musical, *Ziegfeld Girl*.)

Chico entered vaudeville as accompanist for a cousin, Lou Shean. While Lou sang, Chico would play blindfolded. When Lou dropped out, Chico would do a solo act of playing audience requests blindfolded and with a sheet over the keyboard. He then made a living playing the piano in beer gardens and nickelodeons, including one in which he replaced the as yet unknown George Gershwin. He was also song-plugging for music publishers. Minnie decided to form a close harmony act with Harpo, Groucho and Gummo, plus a girl called Janie O'Riley, calling it The Four Nightingales. Harpo was so scared the first time on stage that he wet his pants. Apparently, he sang off-key, while Janie was always missing the high notes. At least Groucho and Gummo could hold a tune.

In the beginning the emphasis was on song, with a smattering of comedy, until the act hit the small town of Nacogdoches, Texas. Half-way through their performance, the entire audience got up and walked out in order to watch a runaway mule. When they returned about thirty minutes later, the brothers were furious and decided to send up their own songs and the audience by firing out insults about Texas and the town with such remarks as, 'Nacogdoches is full of roaches,' The audience, instead of tarring and feathering them, laughed heartily. It was decided that comedy might be their forté.

In Denison, Texas, there was a teachers' convention and Groucho suggested a school routine, the sort of

thing that was popular in vaudeville at the time. So Groucho, Gummo and Harpo concocted a sketch called *Fun in Hi Skule*. Groucho, as Mr Green the angry teacher, put on a German accent, donned a frock coat, and for the first time, wore a fake black moustache. Later he painted one on when he couldn't find a false one. Harpo, as a moronic country bumpkin called Patsy Brannigan, wore a red wig made out of old rope, and blacked out some teeth. Gummo, the best looking of the three, played the straight man. Part of the routine went like this:

Groucho:	If you had ten apples and you wanted to divide them among six people, what would you do?
Harpo:	Make applesauce.
Groucho:	What is the shape of the world?
Harpo:	I don't know.
Groucho:	Well, what shape are my cufflinks
Harpo:	Square.
Groucho:	Not my weekday cufflinks, the ones I wear on Sundays.
Harpo:	Oh. Round.
Groucho:	All right, what is the shape of the world?
Harpo:	Square on weekdays, round on Sundays.

Al Shean wrote a second sketch for them called *Mr Green's Reception*, built around a class reunion, with Groucho as the old teacher whom his former pupils have come back to see. Then Chico left the song-plugging business and joined the act, now called The Marx Brothers and Co.

Shean wrote *Home Again* for the four brothers, a sketch in which Groucho is at the docks having just come off a liner. 'Well, friends, next time I cross the ocean I'll take a train. I'm certainly glad to set my feet on terra firma. Now I know that when I eat something I

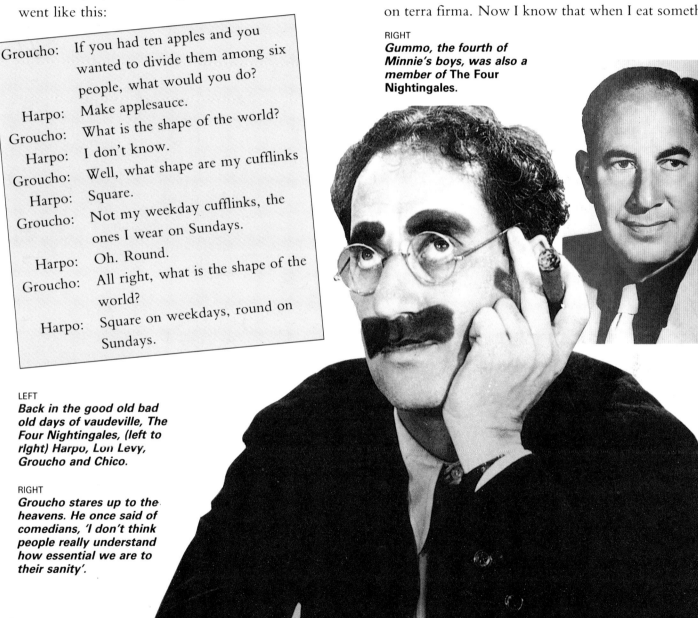

RIGHT
Gummo, the fourth of Minnie's boys, was also a member of The Four Nightingales.

LEFT
Back in the good old bad old days of vaudeville, The Four Nightingales, (left to right) Harpo, Lou Levy, Groucho and Chico.

RIGHT
Groucho stares up to the heavens. He once said of comedians, 'I don't think people really understand how essential we are to their sanity'.

won't see it again.' Gummo played his son, Harpo the bumpkin Patsy Brannigan again, and Chico was Leo the Wop, who steals lingerie from the female passengers. Chico says to Groucho, 'I'd like to say goombye to your wife.' 'Who wouldn't?' he replies. Then Gummo comes out and announces to Groucho, 'Patsy Brannigan the garbage man is here.' 'Tell him we don't want any,' he replies. These jokes were to be reused later in the movies.

It was during *Home Again* that Groucho picked up the idea of wielding a cigar. Other comedians before and after Groucho – George Burns, Robert Woolsey (of Wheeler and Woolsey) – found it a useful stage prop to use while waiting for laughs, or to get laughs, or to gain time if they forgot a line. Groucho dropped the German accent because of the pre-war resentment against anything German, but Chico kept the Italian. Harpo was not particularly good or happy at dialogue and resorted more and more to mime. Gradually, he introduced the taxi horn, the large overcoat with capacious pockets, the battered hat and the red wig. Al Shean bought him a second-hand harp which Harpo practised on for a year before he dared play it on stage. One day, he was involved in a train accident and the harp case was smashed, although the harp remained undamaged. Thinking quickly, Harpo threw the instrument onto the tracks so that it was also broken, and thereby received enough insurance money to buy a new and better one.

As they toured the country, they came across many performers who would become famous, including a violin player in the pit orchestra named Benny Kubelsky, later known as Jack Benny. In Winnipeg and Vancouver they encountered Charlie Chaplin doing his act *A Night at the Club*. They shared the bill with W. C. Fields, with Sarah Bernhardt, and the boxer Benny Leonard. The brothers were earning $1500 a week on the Keith Circuit when vaudeville tycoon E. F. Albee booked them for a week at the Royale on Broadway, prior to a stint at the most famous New York vaudeville theatre of them all, the Palace. Yet after Albee saw their act at the Royale, he expressed dissatisfaction, and wanted to cancel the Palace booking. Minnie, however, forced him to honour the previous commitment. Albee did this but put them in the worst position on the bill – the opening act. They were such a hit with their *Home Again* routine, however, that they were gradually moved to the closing spot. The *Variety* review of 12

February, 1915 said, 'The fun-making is taken care of by three of the Marx brothers. Julius takes the elderly role and is an excellent German comedian. Leonard Marx is the Italian, who plays the piano in trick and other ways, also has comedy scenes with his brother, Arthur Marx. The latter is in what the program says is a nondescript role. This Arthur Marx is marked as a comedian for a Broadway show, just as certain as you are reading this. He is a comedian who doesn't talk. Arthur plays the harp and piano, getting laughs from his handling of both . . . Arthur made the house laugh any time he wanted them to.'

They were yet to use the nicknames by which they would always be known. These evolved during a poker game with the vaudeville monologist Art Fisher, with whom they were sharing a bill in Rockford, Illinois. Fisher kept referring to Julius as Groucho, because of his disposition; Leonard as Chicko, because he always chased chicks, (a typesetter later mistakenly dropped the k from Chicko, and they kept the new spelling); Gummo because he wore gum-soled shoes and could walk up quietly behind people like a gumshoe or private eye; Harpo speaks for itself, although he never did.

Immediately America entered the First World War, Gummo joined up. He had never been particularly comfortable on stage, not only because he didn't have any special talent, but because he had a stammer which surfaced from time to time. Minnie immediately recruited 16-year-old Herbert to replace his soldier brother in the act. Why he was called Zeppo has never been satisfactorily answered, although a critic once

wrote unkindly that he should have been named Zero. Actually, Zeppo was a talented singer and dancer and had as good a sense of humour as his brothers, but he found himself stuck in the role of juvenile straight man for the rest of his career in show business.

The Marx Brothers had played the Palace and had reached the top in vaudeville, so they decided to try their hand at a 'legitimate' musical called *The Cinderella Girl* – 'A Merry Melange of Mirth, Melody and Music.' It played three days in Battle Creek, Michigan during a 'flu epidemic, after which they returned to vaudeville

and *Home Again*, and a new act, *On the Mezzanine*.

In the summer of 1922, during their summer lay-off, Abe Lastfogel, their agent, managed to get them a three-week booking playing *On the Mezzanine* at the huge Coliseum Theatre in London. Unfortunately, they were a terrible flop in London, receiving boos from the audience, as well as being pelted with pennies. Groucho stepped to the footlights and shouted, 'If you people are going to throw coins, I wish to hell you'd throw something a little more substantial – like shillings and guineas.' Although the ad lib brought the house down, it was not sufficient to rescue the act from the jaws of defeat. So they abandoned *On the Mezzanine* and went back to their old standby, *Home Again*, which was a tremendous success.

On their return to the States, they discovered that the tyrannical E. F. Albee was in a rage at their having gone to work in England without his permission. They argued that it hadn't interfered with any work they would have done for Albee, but he insisted that the small print in the contract stipulated that they could not accept jobs elsewhere. As a result, he refused to have them work again on his circuit, and had them black-listed from others. It looked as though the Marx Brothers' stage career was over, a seeming disaster that nonetheless proved to be a blessing in disguise.

LEFT
Gummo and Groucho. Gummo, who left the troupe early, had a stammer that surfaced from time to time.

FROM BROADWAY
TO HOLLYWOOD

Unable to work, the Marx Brothers were beginning to panic. One day, Chico was standing forlornly outside the Palace Theatre when Will Johnstone, the cartoonist of the *New York Evening World*, came across him.

'What are you doing?' asked Johnstone.

'Nothing,' replied Chico, 'and I don't even think I'm allowed to stand here.'

He then told Johnstone the whole sad story of the blacklisting. The cartoonist, who had just written the book for a musical comedy called *Love For Sale*, which had flopped badly, thought it would be a grand idea to build a show around the Marx Brothers and the leftover scenery. Luckily the producer of *Love For Sale*, Joseph M. Gaites, had just met a successful coal dealer who owned a theatre in Philadelphia, which he was willing to let Gaites use. In the meantime, Chico was playing cards with Herman Broody, a wealthy pretzel-salt manufacturer from Hackensack, New Jersey, who was involved with a girl eager to be in a show. Chico agreed to give her a part in the upcoming production and was promptly handed $25,000 to help put it on.

I'll Say She Is consisted mainly of the best routines the Marx Brothers had been using for years, with some new material added. There were twenty-four scenes, including singing and dancing acts, the harp and piano interludes, and a romantic ballad interrupted by Harpo tugging a large cable across the stage to the end of which he himself was tied. In one scene, a detective, congratulating Harpo on his honesty, shakes him by the hand. As he does so, a vast amount of silverware falls out of Harpo's cavernous sleeve, continuing to do so for some minutes, a gag that was to be used again and again in the brothers' films. The finale was a forty-five-minute sketch featuring Groucho as Napoleon, leaving Josephine to go off to battle, and unaware that she has all her lovers hiding in her bedroom.

After running successfully for over four months in Philadelphia, and for almost a year on tour, *I'll Say She Is* opened on Broadway at the Casino Theatre on 19 May, 1924 to excellent reviews, one of them from the acerbic critic Alexander Woollcott of *The New York Sun*: 'As one of the many who laughed immoderately throughout the greater part of *I'll Say She Is*, it behooves your correspondent to report at once that that harlequinade has some of the most comical moments vouchsafed to the first-nighters in a month of Mondays.' He was particularly taken with Harpo: 'Surely there should be dancing in the streets when a great clown.' comes to town, and this man is a great clown,' (Woollcott, the model for Sheridan Whiteside in George S. Kaufman and Moss Hart's play *The Man who Came to Dinner*, became a great advocate of the Marx Brothers and a friend of Harpo's. The character of Banjo, in the same play, was based on Harpo).

Minnie's dream had really come true. While getting dressed to go to the theatre on opening night, she fell off her dressing-table stool in her excitement and broke her leg. Yet, after having it placed in a paster cast, she insisted on being taken in an ambulance from the hospital to the theatre, where she was carried to her seat in the front row just as the curtain went up. There she sat, her encased leg propped up on the rail of the orchestra pit, glowing with maternal pride. It seemed that the years of struggling had finally culminated in glory. Little did she realize that her sons' fame was still in its infancy.

Frenchie Marx, who was sitting beside her, overheard a couple arguing during the interval as to whether the Marxes were real brothers. The wife insisted they were, while her husband claimed they were 'fakes'. The father of the 'fakes' interrupted the discussion by telling the man that he thought he was wrong. The man immediately wanted to bet on it, offering Frenchie odds he could not resist taking.

Not long after the opening Groucho spent six thousand dollars on a seven-seater Lincoln sedan. During a matinée, while Chico was playing his piano solo, and before the Napoleon sketch, Groucho decided

to take the new car for a spin around the block, but found himself stuck in the thick of a traffic jam in his Napoleon outfit. 'Chico had to play fourteen encores,' recalled Groucho. 'And this was pretty difficult, since he only knew ten numbers.'

I'll Say She Is made the Marx Brothers the darlings of the smart set, especially the group of wits that gathered every week around the Round Table at the Algonquin Hotel. Amongst the most famous were Alexander Woollcott, Dorothy Parker, George S. Kaufman, Ring Lardner, Tallulah Bankhead and Robert Benchley. Harpo loved being the centre of attraction, and he would listen to the illustrious intellectuals trying to describe his appeal. Zeppo enjoyed the reflected glory that his older brothers brought him, and Chico got into an exclusive literary poker club known as the Thanatopsis Club. Groucho was less gregarious. 'My idea of a good time is to lock myself in my room with a big Havana and read the *New Yorker*,' he said. By then, he had married the young dancer Ruth Johnson and had a three-year-old son, Arthur.

Now that the brothers were major Broadways stars, a new show was expected from them. This time it would be a real musical-comedy built completely around them, and not just another series of sketches. *The Cocoanuts,* which opened on 8 December 1925, was an even bigger hit than *I'll Say She Is*, running three hundred and seventy seven performances. George Kaufman wrote the book, which lightly satirized the land boom in Florida, and Irving Berlin composed the music. One of the best songs, 'Always', was dropped because Sam Harris, the producer, told Berlin that it wasn't any good. But it was the clowning of the Marx Brothers that the public flocked to see. They seemed to do what they liked with the script as written, adding and

subtracting bits every evening, so that Kaufman was heard to comment, 'Hey, somewhere in the second act I think I heard one of my original lines.'

It was *The Cocoanuts* that introduced the statuesque Margaret Dumont, the woman who was to be the perfect foil for the brothers, especially Groucho, whose 'love scenes' with her are among the highlights of their movies. 'She was practically the fifth Marx Brother,' said Groucho. Whether she played Mrs Claypool or Mrs Rittenhouse, she was always the same society lady, trying to keep her dignity while all around others were losing theirs. Her genuine bemusement at Groucho

added to the amusement. Dumont didn't understand most of the jokes and would ask Groucho, 'What are they laughing about?'

One night, during the run, Harpo asked one of the chorus girls if she would run across the stage in the middle of Groucho's scene with Dumont. It was the beginning of his blonde-chasing gag in which he would dash after them honking his horn. Groucho, unabashed, quipped, 'It's the first time I ever saw a taxi hail a passenger.'

Minnie was more excited about *The Cocoanuts* than anything her sons had done previously. When Groucho

LEFT
'She was practically the fifth Marx Brother.' Margaret Dumont and Groucho Marx in The Cocoanuts (1929), the film that introduced the statuesque actress to the screen. She would appear in seven of the Marx Brothers films,

RIGHT
Harpo at his happiest on screen, surrounded by pretty chorus girls in The Cocoanuts. He would chase any blonde that happened to appear in the films but, unlike older brother Chico, he was more fastidious about women in real life.

asked her what she thought of the show, she replied, 'They laughed a lot, Julius, they laughed a lot.'

Animal Crackers, which followed *The Cocoanuts*, had music by Bert Kalmar and Harry Ruby, and a book by Kaufman and Morrie Ryskind. One radical departure was decided on – the harp and piano solos would be dispensed with. While the show was on the road however, Harpo came up to Ryskind and said, 'Well, Morrie, they love the show all right, but, well, it seems to me it needs something, in the second act somewhere, you know, maybe what they'd like is something aesthetic.' Ryskind knew what he was fishing for and gave way. A few hours later Chico rushed into Ryskind's office. 'What's this about Harpo playing the harp. That sonofabitch touches that harp just once, and I'm gonna do my piano number!' The harp and piano solos were back.

In the autumn of 1928, *Animal Crackers* opened on Broadway, and became their third hit show in a row. Every night, the three brothers – Zeppo was stuck in the straight role – brought in new pieces of script, much to the discomfort of Margaret Dumont, who didn't know from one moment to the next what trick they would play on her, on stage or off.

During the scene when all the guests arrive at Mrs Rittenhouse's palatial home, Harpo is announced and the butler takes his coat, revealing that he has nothing on but swimming trunks. One evening, Harpo forgot to put on the trunks and was revealed to the audience in only his jock-strap. As he ran off the stage embarrassed, Groucho yelled 'Tomorrow night he's not going to wear anything, so get your tickets early!'

The Wall Street crash of 1929 happened during the run of *Animal Crackers*. Groucho, who had invested a great deal in stocks, was wiped out. Harpo lost everything he had and still needed ten thousand dollars to cover debts. Chico never had any money saved, all he ever had he lost at gambling. At least the brothers were earning two thousand dollars a week in *Animal Crackers*, but it was a time, according to Groucho, when 'the pigeons would be feeding the people in Central Park.' Fortunately the film industry was beginning to blossom with the latest innovation – talkies. Producers began looking around for new talent to exploit the medium and, naturally, Broadway was an obvious source for both talent and script material. It was also the time when the visual comedy of Buster Keaton, Charlie Chaplin and Harold Langdon was giving way to the 'comedy of the absurd'.

Paramount signed the brothers for a three-picture contract at seventy-five thousand dollars a picture. The first one was to be *The Cocoanuts*. As *Animal Crackers* was still a Broadway hit, going to Hollywood was out of the question, so it was decided that the film would be made in the spring of 1929 in the Paramount Studios at Astoria, Long Island. It would be possible for the Marx Brothers to do the picture during the day and appear on stage at night. 'Sometimes I'd get so punchy,' recalled Groucho, 'that I'd find myself spouting the dialogue from *Animal Crackers* in a scene I was doing in *Cocoanuts*, and vice versa.'

Actually, it was not the first Marx Brothers experience in front of a camera. They had already made a

FROM LEFT TO RIGHT
Zeppo, Groucho, Chico and Harpo re-enacting their routines from the Broadway stage in The Cocoanuts *for the benefit of the cameras and the primitive sound equipment. The whole picture takes place in a luxury resort hotel in Florida.*

silent movie called *Humor Risk* in 1920, but it was subsequently destroyed, and with good reason! The cheaply-made little film, shot in Fort Lee, New Jersey in between shows, had one showing at a matinée in the Bronx before disappearing for ever. Groucho played the villain, Harpo the hero and Mildred Davis (soon to co-star with Harold Lloyd) the heroine. In 1925, Harpo appeared as the village idiot in a film with Richard Dix called *Too Many Kisses*. Harpo was very excited when the movie was premiered in New York, and told all his friends to go and see it. As he recalled: 'We sat there waiting for me to come on and dominate the screen, and nothing happened at all for a couple of reels.' Just as he bent down to pick up his hat, Minnie cried, 'Look! There you are!' When he looked up he was gone. Most of his role had ended up on the cutting room floor.

The Cocoanuts was one of the earliest sound pictures made in the USA. The equipment kept breaking down and scenes had to be shot over and over again because of extraneous noises being picked up. Nevertheless, the film, however crude, stands as a testimony to what the Marx Brothers and the show were like on stage. Before shooting began, the producer, Walter Wanger, asked Groucho to wear a false moustache rather than his usual painted one because, he said, 'the audience isn't accustomed to anything as phony as that and just won't believe it.' 'The audience doesn't believe us, anyhow,' Groucho replied. 'All they do is laugh at us, and after all, isn't that what we're getting paid for?' Then Wanger offered another warning. 'We can't have you talking directly to the audience, as your habit was on stage.' Groucho's response was to look the producer in the eye and say, 'You, sir, are a schlemiel!' Needless to say, the moustache and asides stayed.

The only thing the co-directors, Joseph Santley and Robert Florey, were required to do was to stick as closely to the original as possible, without opening it out. The French-born Florey, in Hollywood since 1921,

remarked many years later: 'Aside from directing traffic, I photographed it to the best of my ability.'

It was not easy to keep the brothers in line. Groucho kept pestering Florey for French lessons, Harpo would oversleep and Chico would often disappear in order to phone his bookie or join a poker game, and would be late returning for the next scene. The problem was eventually solved by locking him in one of the jail cells being used in the picture. A phone was put in the cell so Chico would be able to lose his money from there. Despite such chaotic conditions, the picture was finished in under a month and opened in New York in May, 1929. When the brothers saw it they wanted to buy up all the negatives and destroy them, but it was a hit with the critics and the public alike.

The plot centred on the Hotel de Cocoanut in Florida, run by Groucho and 'assisted' by Chico and Harpo, where the formidable Margaret Dumont is a guest. Her daughter (Mary Eaton) is in love with the young architect (Oscar Shaw), but the villain (Cyril Ring) plans to steal her mother's diamond necklace, with the help of a conniving woman (Kay Francis), and put the blame on the young man. Zeppo had hardly anything to say or do.

What mattered most was not the soppy romance, with the lovers singing 'The Skies Will All Be Blue When My Dreams Come True' (written for the film by Irving Berlin and certainly not one of his best), nor the silly plot – but the various encounters between Groucho and Dumont, Groucho and Chico, and Harpo and everyone else.

LEFT
Harpo gets the bellboy to hop to it with his honking walking stick at the Hotel de Cocoanut, from where most of the silverware finds its way into Harpo's cavernous pockets. During the shooting of The Cocoanuts, *Harpo would often oversleep and miss his call.*

Groucho
(to Dumont):

Did anyone ever tell you you look like the Prince of Wales? I don't mean the present Prince of Wales. One of the old Wales. And believe me when I say whales, I mean whales. I know a whale when I see one . . . Your eyes – your eyes, they shine like the pants of a blue serge suit.

Dumont: What? The very idea. That's an insult.

Groucho: That's not a reflection on you – it's on the pants . . . One false move and I'm yours. I love you. I love you.

Dumont: I don't think you'd love me if I were poor.

Groucho: I might, but I'd keep my mouth shut.

Hotel manager
Groucho to Chico
arriving as guest:

Hey, hey, do you know that suitcase is empty?

Chico: Thatsa all right. We'll fill it up before we leave.

Groucho explaining to Chico the layout of the area:

And here is a viaduct leading over to the mainland.

Chico: Why a duck?

Groucho: I'm all right. How are you? I say here is a little peninsula and here's a viaduct leading over to the mainland. All right.

Chico: Why a duck? Why-a-no chicken?

The Four Marx Brothers posing for a publicity still for Animal Crackers (1930), which Variety called 'A hit on the screen before it opened, and in the money plenty.' The brothers were not deterred by still-primitive microphone technique, and the jokes came across loud and clear.

Harpo, of course, ran through the picture stealing everything in sight.

The Cocoanuts turned out to be the last of her sons' shows that Minnie saw. She died at the age of sixty-five on 13 September 1929, when they were preparing to take *Animal Crackers* on tour. She suffered a stroke following a family party and died during the night. Harpo remembered: 'She was trying to say something. I knew what she was trying to say. I reached over and straightened her wig, the new blond wig she had bought especially for tonight. The smile came back for a second. Then it faded, and all the life in Minnie faded with it. I took her into my arms. I don't remember what I said, or thought. I only remember I was crying.'

Minnie had lived to see the start of a film career and

international stardom beyond anything she had dreamed of for them. Her last years had been spent happily and comfortably with Frenchie in their house in Little Neck, New York, which their sons had bought them. They had a car and chauffeur and no more financial worries ever again.

Following the success of *The Cocoanuts*, it was time to put *Animal Crackers* on the screen. Again they invaded Paramount's Astoria studios, but sound techniques had advanced somewhat in ten months and their second talkie was better than their first. As with the stage show, the music was by Bert Kalmar and Harry Ruby, but the script by Morrie Ryskind without George

OVERLEAF
Scenes from Animal Crackers, *Groucho as Captain Spaulding, bogus African explorer, wooing Mrs Rittenhouse, in the statuesque shape of Margaret Dumont; a musical soirée enlivened by Chico and Harpo at the piano.*

RIGHT
Harpo and Chico confuse self-styled art expert Abie the fishmonger (Louis Sorin) in the plot which involved a stolen painting.

Kaufman. The director, Victor Heerman, who had been warned about the difficulty of getting the four of them on the set at the same time and of their disappearances, was determined to get the brothers to toe the line. An assistant director was assigned to look after each brother, and be answerable for their whereabouts. Nevertheless, Lillian Roth, who played the ingenue, called the set 'one step removed from a circus.' The singer, later portrayed by Susan Hayward in *I'll Cry Tomorrow*, had been sent East to teach her a lesson for having given Cecil B. DeMille a lot of trouble on *Madame Satan*.

Animal Crackers is set on a large estate belonging to the redoubtable Mrs Rittenhouse (Margaret Dumont, of course). The plot revolves round the theft of a valuable painting, which her daughter wishes to substitute with a copy made by her artist boyfriend in the hope that he will be given acclaim. The name of Rittenhouse came from a hotel in Philadelphia, and from then on Dumont was always affectionately called Mrs Rittenhouse by

the Marx Brothers offscreen.

In the movie Groucho makes his most famous entrance, as Captain Spaulding, an African explorer. Dressed in boots, riding pants and a pith helmet, he is carried onto the set sitting in a bamboo and tiger-skin sedan chair borne by four Nubian warriors. The chorus sings 'Hooray for Captain Spaulding,' to which he replies in song, 'Hello, I must be going – I cannot stay I came to say I must be going – I'm glad I came but just the same I must be going.' He then does an eccentric dance and recounts his adventures to the assembled company.

'Up at six, breakfast at six-thirty, and back to bed at seven . . . One morning I shot an elephant in my pyjamas. How he got into my pyjamas I'll never know. Then we tried to remove the tusks, but they were embedded so firmly that we couldn't budge them. Of course, in Alabama the Tuskaloosa. But that's entirely irrelephant.'

At one moment Groucho faces the camera and says, 'Well, *all* the jokes can't be good! You've got to expect that once in a while!' The film also contains a parody of Eugene O'Neill's *Strange Interlude*. The joke seems intellectual nowadays, but most American audiences knew about the interior monologues in the then current Broadway play.

Harpo goes through his wonderful routine of blowing bubbles that turn out to be cigarette smoke, hanging his leg on someone's arm, dropping silverware from his vast sleeves, preparing to punch someone with the left hand while delivering with the right, wrapping himself around Chico, and playing the harp. During a bridge game which he and Chico play with Dumont and a partner, he cheats blissfully and throws away or rips up any card he dislikes.

Animal Crackers opened in New York in August 1930 to even better reviews than *The Cocoanuts*, but the boys were yet to make a picture that was not a static filming of a stage success. It was time for the Marx Brothers to move on into original material, to leave New York and make for Hollywood.

HOORAY FOR FREEDONIA!

4

Towards the end of 1930, the Marx Brothers needed a change. They had been on Broadway and on the road for over seven years, as well as having made two new films at the same time. The death of their mother the year before lay heavy on them, and they still had not recovered from the Wall Street crash. The prospect of making a new start in Hollywood was a rosy one. Before leaving for California, they accepted an offer to appear for six weeks in a Charles Cochran revue at the Palace Theatre in London, where they would do a mixture of their best comedy routines.

Groucho with Ruth and their children, Arthur and Miriam; Chico with his wife Betty (they left their daughter Maxine in New York); Zeppo and his wife, and Harpo, who was still a bachelor, crossed to Europe on the French liner, the *Paris*. They found the welcome much warmer than when they were first in England at the Coliseum in 1922. British audiences were now familiar with their antics from the film versions of *The Cocoanuts* and *Animal Crackers*, and greeted them with much laughter and applause.

When they arrived back in the States on 14 February, 1931, the brothers were asked by a radio network to do a series. (Harpo on the radio!) So before carrying out their film commitment to Paramount, the four brothers met a couple of writers, Will B. Johnstone, who had written *I'll Say She Is*, and S. J. Perelman, then primarily a cartoonist, at the Astor Hotel to talk about ideas for the radio show. For a long time the discussion was non-productive. Chico kept excusing himself to go and call the race track. Harpo kept getting up and holding conversations with young ladies. Groucho dismissed anything the others suggested. Suddenly, Johnstone burst out, 'Stowaways on an ocean liner.' The brothers, with memories fresh from their crossing of the Atlantic, thought it a great basis for their first Hollywood movie

*(Anticlockwise) Groucho
(shading his eyes), Solly
Violinsky, S.J. Perelman,
Will B. Johnstone, Arthur
Sheekman.*

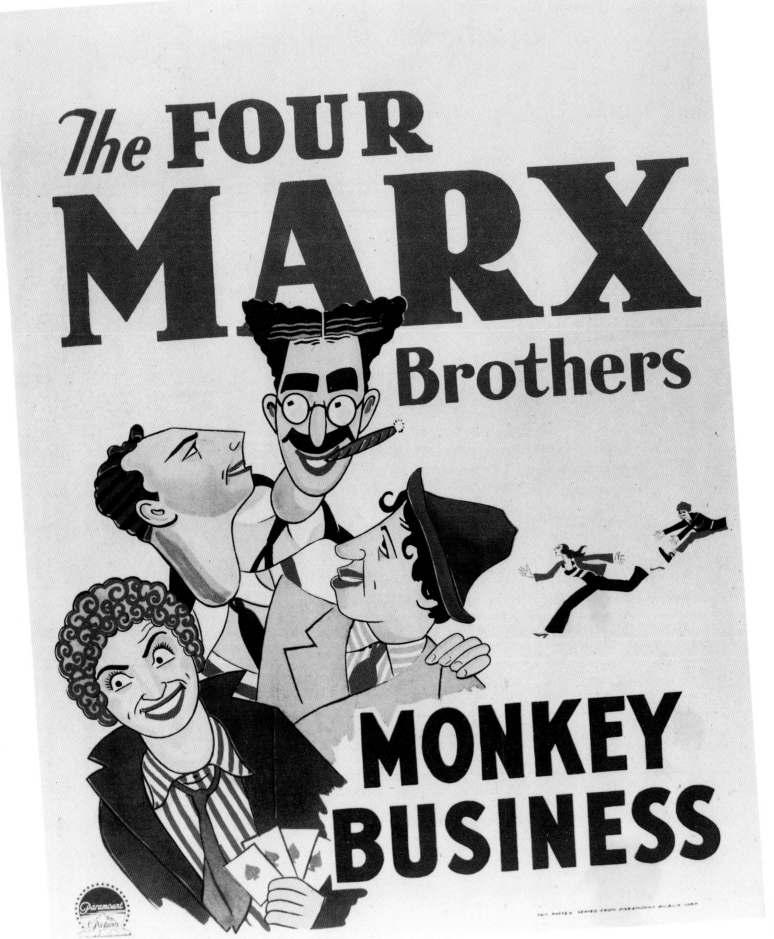

and abandoned the idea of doing the radio series.

The Marx Brothers took to the Californian life-style immediately. Chico spent most of his free time at the Santa Ana race track; Harpo, who lived at the Garden of Allah, enjoyed going to parties. Groucho loved the climate above all. He never went Hollywood – seldom attended parties, never went to premiers, refused to leave his handprint in cement outside Grauman's Chinese Theatre and resisted installing a swimming-pool, much to the annoyance of his children.

For *Monkey Business*, the first original Marx Brothers screenplay, Jesse Lasky, Paramount's head of production, hired Will Johnstone and S. J. Perelman, as well as appointing a gag man for each of them – Arthur Sheekman, a Chicago newspaper columnist for Groucho; Nat Perrin, a law student with writing aspirations for Chico; and for Harpo, J. Carver Pusey, the author of a comic strip called Little Benny, about a boy unable to speak. Groucho greeted the result of their combined labours with, 'It stinks!'. A new script included cracks Groucho had made to the captain on board the *Paris*.

Groucho:	I don't care for the way you're running this boat. Why don't you get in the back seat for a while and let your wife drive?
Captain:	I want you to know I've been captain of this ship for twenty-two years.
Groucho:	Twenty-two years, eh? If you were a man you'd go into business for yourself. I knew a fella started only last year with just a canoe. Now he's got more women than you can shake a stick at, if that's your idea of a good time.
Captain:	One more word out of you and I'll throw you in irons!
Groucho:	You can't do it with irons, it's a mashie shot. It's a mashie shot if the wind's against you, and if the wind isn't, I am!

Nat Perrin's main contribution to the script was the line, 'Atsa fine, boss,' for Chico, which he continued to use throughout his career, especially when he couldn't think of what he was supposed to say. Keeping the brothers in order were producer Herman J. Mankiewicz and the softly spoken director Norman McLeod, who once described himself as 'quiet as a mouse pissing on a blotter.'

Sadly missing from the cast (and from the following film) was Margaret Dumont. The story required a sexy temptress to act as Groucho's foil, not a high society dame. This was splendidly provided by blonde comedienne Thelma Todd, who had often mixed it with Laurel and Hardy. 'You're awfully shy for a lawyer,' she tells Groucho. 'You bet I'm shy. I'm a shyster lawyer,' he replies. Frenchie, the brothers' father, was used as an extra, the only time he ever appeared in a film. He got twelve-and-a-half dollars a day and worked for two days. He appears twice, once on the ship before the

 ABOVE
The musical interludes sometimes slowed up the movies, but Harpo's solos revealed his serious side.

OVERLEAF
On the set of Monkey Business *(1931), directed by Norman Z. McLeod (seated centre, holding cigarette).*

interview with an opera celebrity, who is referred to as Madame Frenchie, and once on the dock. He is the dapper gentleman standing behind his sons as they wave to the camera.

We first see the brothers in *Monkey Business* popping out of four barrels on board ship, implying correctly that they are going to be a barrelful of fun. As stowaways, they spend most of their time running amok about the liner, avoiding the crew, getting involved with gangsters, and insulting the passengers. Only Zeppo slows down somewhat by providing the slight love interest. Harpo, when not chasing blondes, is being chased by the first mate. Once he eludes his pursuer by disguising himself as a puppet in a Punch and Judy show. Harpo and Chico also take over the barber shop, giving a customer the works. In one of their funniest scenes, the brothers steal a passport so they can get off the ship and enter America. But whose passport do they steal? That of Maurice Chevalier! Surrealistically, they try to convince the immigration officials that they are Chevalier by singing, in turn, one

of his hit songs, 'You Brought a New Kind of Love to Me'. The song had featured in the Paramount movie, *The Big Pond*, the year before. Harpo is the most successful when he mimes to a Chevelier record on a gramophone strapped to his back, until it runs down. The movie does the same once it gets onto dry land, proving how difficult it was for screenwriters to fit the anarchic brothers into a conventional plot structure. However, there were enough comic gems before the lame climax to make *Monkey Business* one of the biggest hits of the season. As a result, Paramount signed the Marx Brothers for two more films, at two hundred thousand dollars a picture.

Many years later, during World War II, Churchill wrote in his memoirs: 'After dinner, news arrived of the heavy raid on London. There was nothing that I could do about it so I watched the Marx Bros in a comic film which my hosts had arranged. I went out twice to inquire about the air raid and heard it was bad. The merry film clacked on, and I was glad of the diversion.' The 'merry film' was *Monkey Business*.

Blonde Thelma Todd replaced Margaret Dumont as Groucho's inamorata in Monkey Business, *because the plot required a sexy temptress rather than a high society woman.*

The Four Marx Brothers
(right) as stowaways at
the opening of Monkey
Business, *most of the
action of which takes
place on board a liner. The
first of their pictures
written especially for the
screen included a scene
(below) in which Chico
and Harpo become demon
barbers, and (bottom)
Groucho crashes a society
party. The movie was less
good when it reached dry
land.*

Adolph Zukor presents

THE 4 MARX BROTHERS

"Horse Feathers"

DIRECTED BY NORMAN McLEOD

A PARAMOUNT PICTURE

For *Horse Feathers* (1932), the musical numbers were provided by Bert Kalmar and Harry Ruby, who also wrote the script with S. J. Perlman and Will B. Johnstone. Norman McLeod directed once more, and Thelma Todd played the attractive 'college widow' with whom Zeppo, as Groucho's son, is in love. Zeppo had complained that all he ever did was announce Groucho at a party, so he was given the romantic lead, and got to sing a soppy ballad, 'Everyone Says I Love You.'

Groucho as Professor Quincy Adams Wagstaff, Dean of Huxley College, sings 'Whatever It Is I'm Against It,' an anarchic anthem that certainly proclaims him a non-conformist. He then proceeds to puncture the pomposity of his colleagues and display a healthy philistinism.

| Professor: | The absorption of oxygen into the blood is taking place every moment of our waking and sleeping hours. |
| Groucho: | Excepting February, which has twenty-eight, and every leap year one day more. |

RIGHT
David Landau and Thelma Todd do some plotting while Chico, Groucho and Harpo do some eaves-dropping in Horse
Feathers (1932), one of their funniest films. Thelma Todd died prematurely in suspicious circumstances in 1936 aged 31.

1376-43

Groucho then spots Zeppo sitting in the auditorium with a girl on his lap. 'Young lady,' he says. 'Would you mind getting up so I could see the son rise? . . . I'd horsewhip you if I had a horse!'

Huxley college hasn't won a football match since it was founded in 1888, and Groucho is forced to do something about improving the team. Knowing of the illegal practice of buying pro football players to play for a college, Zeppo tells him he can buy two of the greatest players in the country, who hang out at a speakeasy downtown. Groucho hastens to the dive only to be confronted by the moronic Chico at the door, and one of their funniest routines ensues.

Chico: You can't come in unless you give the password.
Groucho: Well, what is the password?
Chico: Aw no! You gotta tell *me*. Hey, I tell what I do. I give you three guesses . . . It's the name of a fish.
Groucho: Is it Mary?
Chico: Ha, ha! Atsa no fish!
Groucho: She isn't, well, she drinks like one. Let me see . . . Is it sturgeon?
Chico: Ah, you crazy, sturgeon he's a doctor, cuts you open whenna you sick . . . Now I give you one more chance.
Groucho: I got it! Haddock!
Chico: Atsa funny, I gotta haddock too . . . You can't come in here unless you say swordfish! Now I give you one more guess.
Groucho: Swordfish . . . I think I got it. Is it swordfish?
Chico: Ha! At's it! You guess it!
Groucho: Pretty good, eh?

Chico and Harpo are kept prisoners in their underwear by two goons (one of them Nat Pembleton, centre) in Horse Feathers, to stop them getting to the football game.

Finally, Groucho manages to buy the pros in time for the big game against Darwin College. (The academic joke here – Darwin vs Huxley – might have been lost on much of the audience.) He is seduced by Thelma Holt however, a spy for Darwin, because he has the football signals. To cut a long pair of pants short, on the day of the game, Chico and Harpo are prisoners in their underwear after being kidnapped. They manage to escape in time, arriving on the field by horse-cart like Ben Hur in his chariot. Huxley win by a vast score thanks to the Marx Brothers' total disregard for the rules, (something which happened on almost every sporting occasion). Funny as it is, the knockabout humour of the finale in all their films is not nearly as telling or amusing as Groucho's verbal felicities, Chico's verbal infelicities, and Harpo's non-verbal felicities.

Of the latter, Harpo, as a dog catcher, has a hilarious scene with a cop, which ends up with the officer locked up in the wagon with the dogs. Harpo also has a wonderful time with slot machines, a pay telephone, and a trolley conductor's change belt, all of which pay out the jackpot, as well as cutting a pack of cards in his own special way – with an axe!

Horse Feathers got the brothers on the cover of *Time Magazine*, and made the members of the surrealist movement in Paris drool. Salvador Dali wrote a script called *The Marx Brothers on Horseback Salad*, decorated with sketches, and made a barbed wire harp tuned with spoons, which he presented to Harpo in Hollywood. Harpo was among William Randolph Hearst's glittering guests at San Simeon, while Groucho was happy in the company of other comedians – Will Rogers, W. C. Fields and Charlie Chaplin. The latter, whom the brothers had met on the vaudeville circuit many years

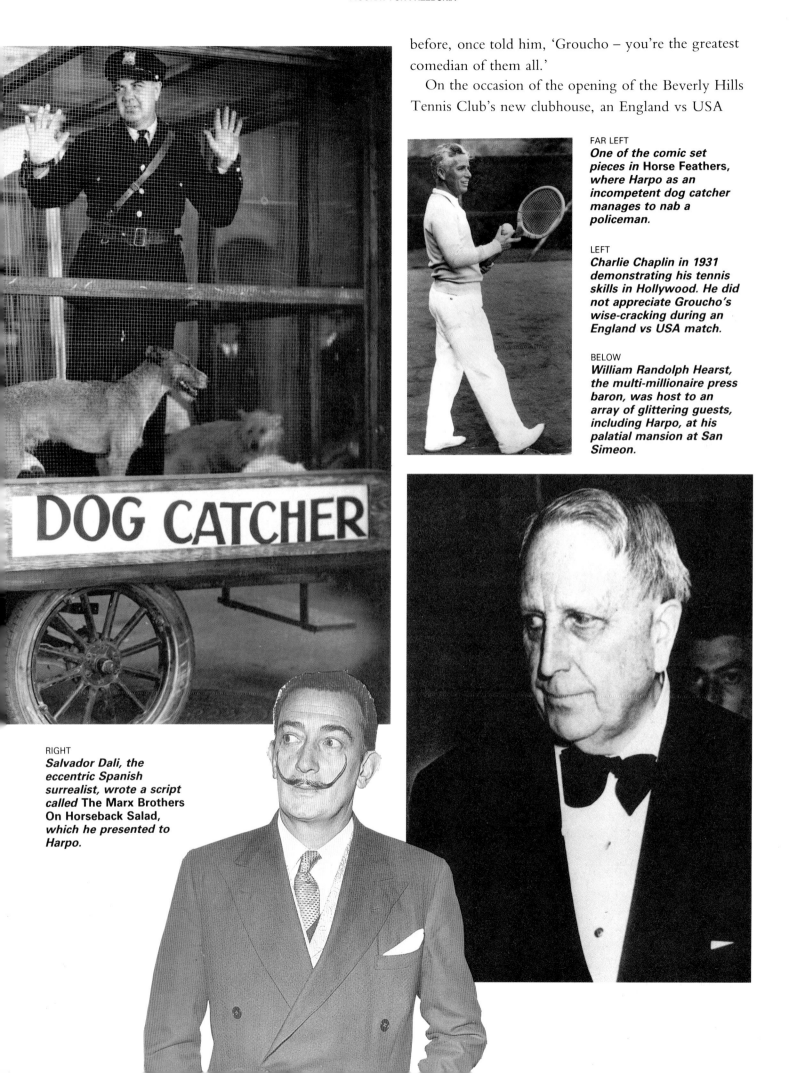

before, once told him, 'Groucho – you're the greatest comedian of them all.'

On the occasion of the opening of the Beverly Hills Tennis Club's new clubhouse, an England vs USA

FAR LEFT
One of the comic set pieces in **Horse Feathers**, *where Harpo as an incompetent dog catcher manages to nab a policeman.*

LEFT
Charlie Chaplin in 1931 demonstrating his tennis skills in Hollywood. He did not appreciate Groucho's wise-cracking during an England vs USA match.

BELOW
William Randolph Hearst, the multi-millionaire press baron, was host to an array of glittering guests, including Harpo, at his palatial mansion at San Simeon.

RIGHT
Salvador Dali, the eccentric Spanish surrealist, wrote a script called **The Marx Brothers On Horseback Salad**, *which he presented to Harpo.*

DOG CATCHER

tennis doubles match was arranged. Groucho was paired with champion Ellsworth Vines against Chaplin and British Wimbledon winner Fred Perry. Groucho, who arrived with twelve rackets, kept distracting Chaplin's attention with his wisecracks. Finally, Charlie, who took his tennis seriously, burst out, 'I didn't come here to be your straight man!'

With the rise of Fascism in Europe and talk of hostilities, it seemed the right time for Hollywood to make an anti-war satire, and who better to do it than the Marx Brothers? On this occasion, they decided to choose their own director. Leo McCarey, who had been connected with Laurel and Hardy as writer, director and producer from 1927 to 1931, had so impressed the brothers with his direction of the Eddie Cantor musical *The Kid from Spain* (1932), that they wanted him to steer them through *Duck Soup*.

The title – explained by Groucho thus: 'Take two

ABOVE
Groucho, wife Ruth, son Arthur, daugher Miriam, brother Harpo, and chimpanzee (no relation) in happy pre-war days.

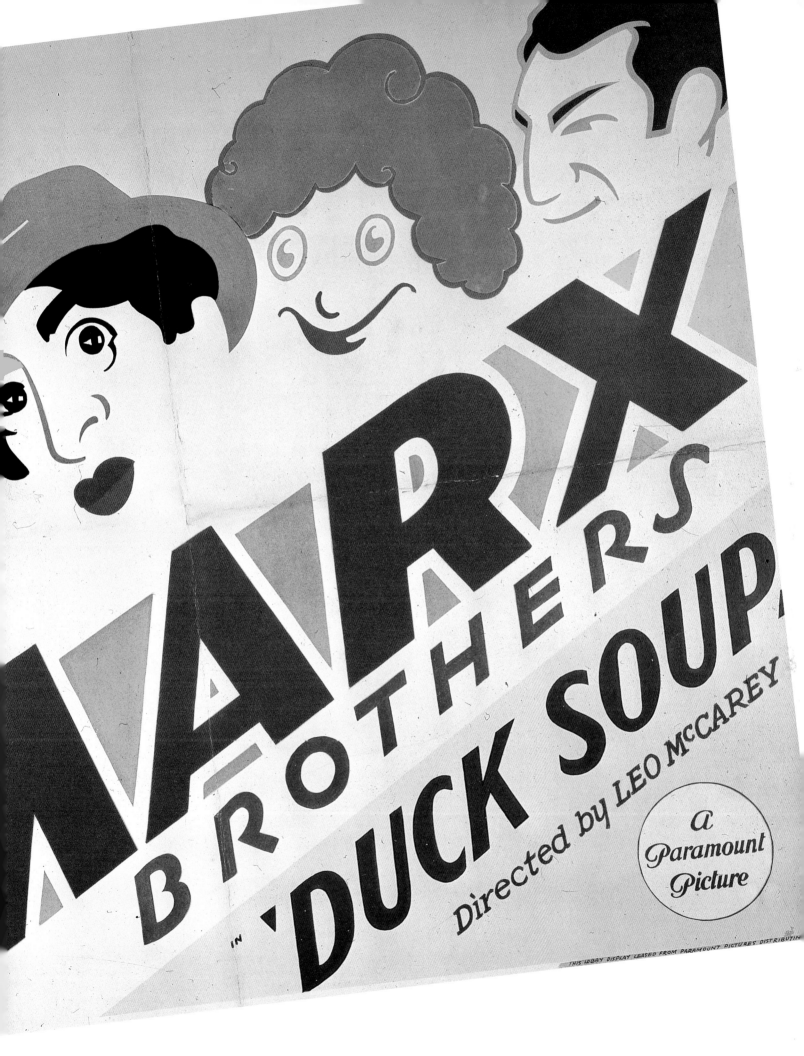

MARX BROTHERS in 'DUCK SOUP'

Directed by LEO McCAREY

A Paramount Picture

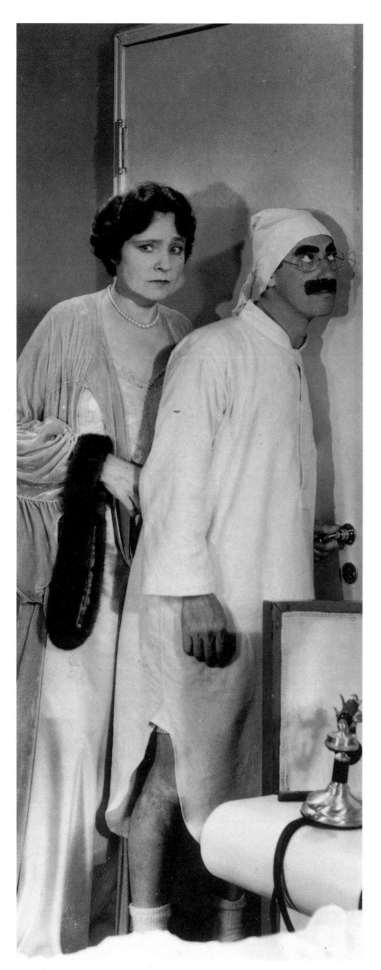

turkeys, one goose, four cabbages, but no duck, and mix them together. After one taste, you'll duck soup the rest of your life' – had been used for a 1927 Laurel and Hardy short. The film contains a hilarious encounter between Harpo and Laurel and Hardy stalwart, Edgar Kennedy, that is reminiscent of the comedy duo at their best. Kennedy, as a lemonade vendor, has a silent tit-for-tat confrontation with Harpo, who is selling peanuts on the same spot. Harpo burns Kennedy's hat, Kennedy turns over the peanut stand, Harpo wades up to his knees in the lemonade.

Most of *Duck Soup* however ventured into new absurdist territory. It is set in the mythical kingdom of Freedonia, which has Groucho as Rufus T. Firefly, the dictator, elected by the wealthy Mrs Teasdale (Margaret Dumont, thankfully back in the fold), Chico as minister of war, Harpo as Groucho's chauffeur, and Zeppo as Groucho's secretary. Chico and Harpo are also spies for Trentino (Louis Calhern), Groucho's political rival.

Dumont:	The future of Freedonia rests on you. Promise me you'll follow in footsteps of my husband.
Groucho:	How do you like that? I haven't been on the job five minutes and already she's making advances to me. Not that I care. Where is your husband?
Dumont:	Why he's dead.
Groucho:	I bet he's just using that as an excuse.
Dumont:	I was with him to the very end.
Groucho:	Huh! No wonder he passed away.
Dumont:	I held him in my arms and kissed him.
Groucho:	Oh, I see. Then it was murder.

LEFT
Groucho, in cotton nightcap and long night shirt, caught in what appears to be a compromising situation with Margaret Dumont in Duck Soup *(1933).*

RIGHT
Peanut seller Harpo and lemonade vendor Edgar Kennedy find themselves at loggerheads in Duck Soup. *Kennedy, master of the slow burn, was often a foil of Laurel and Hardy's.*

The film is crowded with classic Marx Brothers routines, without being interrupted by the bane of many fans – piano and harp solos and young love stuff (a romance between Zeppo and Raquel Torres was mercifully cut). Never had the team been more demonic. Witness the scene where Harpo and Chico enter Trentino's office armed with blowtorches, mousetraps, alarm clocks and phonograph records, and nothing is safe from Harpo's wielding of a pair of scissors. The highlight of the picture, however, is the celebrated mirror scene. While Chico and Harpo have made a nocturnal entry into the villa to steal the national

At the ball given by Mrs Teasdale (Dumont), Freedonia's wealthiest woman, Groucho, as Rufus T. Firefly makes his entrance to the strains of 'His Excellency Is Due' in **Duck Soup**, *the film most fans consider their masterpiece.*

defence plans, the large mirror in the salon gets broken. Groucho, dressed in a cotton nightcap and long nightshirt, is woken and investigates the noise. Chico and Harpo disguise themselves as Groucho, so there are three Grouchos running around the villa. When Groucho looks into what he takes to be a mirror, he sees Chico as his reflection. They play a game, trying to catch each other out, and end up exchanging positions and passing through the imaginary mirror.

Finally war breaks out – 'There must be a war. I've paid a month's rent on the battlefield' – and comic insanity breaks loose. Groucho fires on his own troops, and when Zeppo points this out, Groucho says, 'Here's five dollars. Keep it under your hat. Never mind, I'll keep it under *my* hat.' The tempo accelerates until Mrs Teasdale – 'Remember we're fighting for this woman's honour, which is probably more than *she* ever did' – launches into a full-throated song of victory, and the brothers bombard her with apples.

Duck Soup, now considered by most Marxians as their master piece, was surprisingly ill received when it was released in 1933. *The New York Times* thought it 'extremely noisy without being nearly as mirthful as their other films,' and the *New York Sun* commented that the Marx Brothers had taken 'something of a nose dive.' After World War II, the Korean War and the Vietnam War, *Duck Soup* seems not only funnier but more satiric than it did to pre-war audiences. Mind you, it was sharp enough at the time to have been banned in Italy by Mussolini – a fact which filled the brothers with immense pride. (All their films were banned in Germany because the Marxes were Jewish.)

Shortly after the film's release, Paramount received a letter from a town in New York State called Fredonia. It read: 'The name of Fredonia has been without blot since 1817. I feel it is my duty as mayor to question your intentions in using the name of our city in your picture.' Groucho replied in writing. 'Your Excellency: Our advice is that you change the name of your town. It is hurting our picture. Anyhow, what makes you think you're Mayor of Fredonia? Do you wear a black moustache, play a harp, speak with an Italian accent or chase girls like Harpo? We are certain you do not. Therefore, we must be Mayor of Fredonia, not you. The old gray Mayor ain't what he used to be.'

ABOVE
The satirical barbs against totalitarian regimes and senseless wars in Duck Soup *were powerful enough for Italian fascist dictator Benito Mussolini, pictured here in 1943, to have the film banned in Italy.*

METRO GOLDWYN MARX

The mixed reviews that greeted *Duck Soup* and the mediocre box-office takings put the Marxes in an awkward position when it came to re-negotiating their Paramount contract. Nineteen thirty-three was the worst year in the history of the studio, which was forced to file for bankruptcy. In the same year, Frenchie Marx went into hospital and, after flirting with the nurses for a while, breathed his last on 11 May.

The brothers announced they were forming a new company with stage producer Sam Harris, but this fell through. Then Paramount decided not to renew their contract, and Groucho spearheaded a movement to form a Screen Actors' Guild. At the same time, Zeppo decided it was time for him to quit as a performer because he was fed up with being merely the extra brother and having nothing much to do, as well as bearing the brunt of jokes made about his ineffectiveness. So the youngest Marx brother became a Hollywood agent with Orsatti and Brene, later setting up on his own with Gummo, the second youngest, who had been in the clothing business in New York.

Among their clients were the two celebrated married couples, Clark Gable and Carole Lombard, and Robert Taylor and Barbara Stanwyck. When the agency was ultimately sold to MCA, Zeppo continued to pursue his other business interests, which included racing thoroughbred horses, manufacturing a special type of gasket bought by an aircraft company, and later patenting a special wristwatch for monitoring the functioning of the heart.

Gummo told the story of his own lack of fame. 'When my son was six years old and in school, he came home quite excited one day. My wife asked how school was and he explained that school was fine and that he told everyone that his daddy was one of the Marx Bros . . . "I told them I was Harpo's son." "Why did you say that?" asked my wife. "Why didn't you say you were Gummo Marx's son?" "Well," he said, "who's ever heard of Gummo Marx?" '

With no films in the offing, Groucho and Chico decided to do a radio show called *Flywheel, Shyster and Flywheel*, which started in February 1934. The extremely funny half-hour episodes were written alternately by Arthur Sheekman, Nat Perrin, George Oppenheimer and Tom McKnight, and were about a shyster lawyer (Groucho) and his incompetent assistant Ravelli (Chico). It ran twenty-six weeks until the sponsors, Standard Oil of New Jersey, cancelled the show.

Following the radio series, Groucho decided to take his family for a long vacation in Maine. Directly across the lake from the eight-room cottage was the Lakewood Playhouse, a summer stock repertory troupe. When he was asked by them to play the lead in Ben Hecht and

Charles MacArthur's *Twentieth Century*, Groucho jumped at the chance. In a show that was not a Marx Brothers vehicle for the first time, Groucho was impressive in the role of the temperamental Broadway producer (played by John Barrymore in the film of the same year). 'What a racket this straight acting is!' he told his wife after the first performance. 'Anyone can do it. It doesn't take any talent at all.' His comparison was with the tough challenge of being a comedian. 'When you come out on the stage in funny clothes and funny make-up, the audience unconsciously sets up a resistance to you. Right away their attitude is: so you're a comedian? Well, let's see how funny you can be. Go ahead. Make me laugh. I dare you to. But when you come out in street clothes and look like a normal human being, they don't expect to be in the aisles at the first word you say. When you do say something funny, they're pleasantly surprised and laugh all the harder.' It is quite likely that had Chico not struck up a card-playing friendship with MGM production head, Irving Thalberg, Groucho might have gone into straight acting, and the Marx Brothers would have broken up for ever.

While Groucho was in Maine, and Harpo was a guest of the Soviet Union, where he played the Leningrad

LEFT
Irving G. Thalberg, the 'Boy Wonder' of Hollywood, who became head of production at MGM at the age of 25. It was he who got the Marx Brothers to sign with MGM after the financial disaster of Duck Soup *at Paramount.*

RIGHT
Between pictures, Groucho and Chico did a series of half-hour radio shows called Flywheel, Shyster And Flywheel in 1934. Neither Zeppo (centre) nor Harpo, for obvious reasons, took part.

music hall, Chico remained in Hollywood on the lookout for new opportunities. During a bridge game with Chico, Thalberg had expressed interest in the brothers, and he arranged to meet all three for lunch to discuss a deal. In the autumn of 1934, Harpo, Chico and Groucho met the 'boy wonder' at the Beverly Wilshire.

RIGHT
The Three Marx Brothers, now free of Zeppo, give out in song in a publicity still for A Night At The Opera (1935), their first film for MGM and their biggest hit.

BELOW
Zeppo, the youngest Marx Brother, decided to quit the movies and set up as a Hollywood agent. He was fed up with the jokes about his lack of talent.

Thalberg, who noticed Zeppo was missing from the conference, asked if the three of them would want to be paid as much as four had. 'Don't be silly,' answered Groucho. 'Without Zeppo we're worth twice as much.' Then Thalberg was asked how he liked their Paramount pictures. He thought they were not bad, but not good either. Groucho took offence, but Harpo and Chico tried to calm him, realising he might be biting the hand that was to feed them. Thalberg then explained his theories and how he thought they could make very profitable movies together. 'They were very funny pictures,' he expounded. 'The trouble was they had no stories. It's better to be not so funny and have a story that the audience is interested in. I don't agree with the principle: anything for a laugh. For my money, comedy scenes have to further the plot. They have to be helping someone who's a sympathetic character. With a sound story, your pictures would be twice as good and you'd gross three times as much.' Despite their qualms as to how their knockabout comedy would fit into Thalberg's concept, they knew the thirty-five-year old Thalberg was no fool, and when he offered them fifteen percent of the gross profits on two pictures, unheard of in those days, a deal was struck.

There are many stories of the practical jokes the brothers used to play on Thalberg. The MGM executive was well known for keeping people waiting, so, after the Marxes had been waiting in an outer office for almost an hour, they lit three big cigars and blew the smoke under Thalberg's door. Thinking the place was on fire, he rushed out and they rushed into his office. Thalberg was also in the habit of leaving in the middle of a meeting and coming back later. When he returned from one of his long absences, he was greeted by the brothers stark naked, roasting potatoes on a fire in the grate.

There was a lot of kidding around the MGM lot. Once Groucho and Harpo came across Garbo under a large hat and glasses. Harpo peeped under the hat to see who it was. 'Excuse us,' said Groucho, 'I thought you were a fellow I once knew in Pittsburgh.'

But during the making of the pictures, there was little time for pranks. For their first MGM movie, James K. McGuinness came up with a story line in which the Marxes would wreak havoc in the dignified atmosphere of the Metropolitan Opera House. To write the script,

Thalberg, at the brothers' wish, hired their previous writers George S. Kaufman and Morrie Ryskind, and also Al Boasberg, a larger-than-life gag writer, who worked a lot for Jack Benny. After seeing the completed scenario for *A Night at the Opera* however, the threesome still felt uneasy because they were particularly sensitive after the Paramount sacking. They reflected that *The Cocoanuts* and *Animal Crackers* were their best shows because they had played them on the stage first and discovered what audiences found funny or not, and therefore had time to hone their routines according to the response. To pacify his stars, Thalberg suggested they go on a six-week tour of Salt Lake City, Seattle, Portland and Santa Barbara, trying out the material in front of live audiences before shooting began. What are now classic moments were a result of trial and error on the road during the spring of 1935.

For example, the best remembered sequence out of all the Marx Brothers movies, the stateroom scene, was almost cut out, because it was failing to get laughs. Luckily, they decided to give it one more chance. 'So this night we did it our way,' wrote Harpo in his autobiography *Harpo Speaks!* 'Groucho, ordering a meal from a steward while being jostled into a corner of the jammed-up stateroom, said, "And a hard-boiled egg." I honked my horn. "Make it two hard-boiled eggs," said Groucho. The audience broke up, and as simply as that, a dud became a classic.'

When it came to filming, the brothers did not appreciate the director, Sam Wood, who insisted on multiple takes. 'This jerk we have for a director doesn't

Greta Garbo was at the height of her Hollywood career when the Marx Brothers appeared on the MGM lot. Despite her gloomy screen persona, the Swedish star enjoyed a laugh.

Aboard a luxury liner, people crowd into Groucho's tiny cabin, including two maids, two plumbers, a manicurist and stowaways Chico, Harpo and Allan Jones (centre) who emerge from a huge trunk, in the celebrated stateroom scene from A Night At The Opera.

859-10

*Fiorello (Chico) gets
friendly with the
manicurist and Tomasso
(Harpo) sleeps on his feet
in the birdcage-sized
cabin of Otis B. Driftwood
(Groucho). When Mrs
Claypool (Margaret
Dumont) opens the door,
the crowd, which includes
someone looking for her
Aunt Minnie, spills out at
her feet.*

know what he wants so he shoots everything twenty times and hopes there's something good in it,' commented Groucho. Harpo had to hang onto a ship's rope (which he was swinging on to peer into the portholes), for so long that his hands began to bleed. Wood also imposed a fifty-dollar fine on anybody who came late, a penalty that was especially costly for Chico.

A Night at the Opera opens in Milan where Groucho as Otis B. Driftwood tells the wealthy Mrs Claypool (Margaret Dumont, who else?) that if she invests her money in an opera company, he will introduce her to New York society. Driftwood signs up singers Rosa Castaldi (Kitty Carlisle) and egomaniacal Rodolfo Lassparri (Woolf King). Harpo is Lassparri's ill-treated dresser, and Chico, a dubious agent, who represents tenor Riccardo Baroni (Allan Jones, in a bigger and better Zeppo-type role). Baroni is in love with Rosa.

In Driftwood's tiny cabin on board the liner bound for New York are Groucho, and a huge trunk containing stowaways Chico, Harpo and Allan Jones. In quick succession arrive two maids to make up the beds, an engineer and his assistant to turn off the heat, a manicurist, someone looking for her Aunt Minnie, a cleaning woman, and a troop of waiters bringing dinner. When Dumont opens the door, everything and everyone falls out.

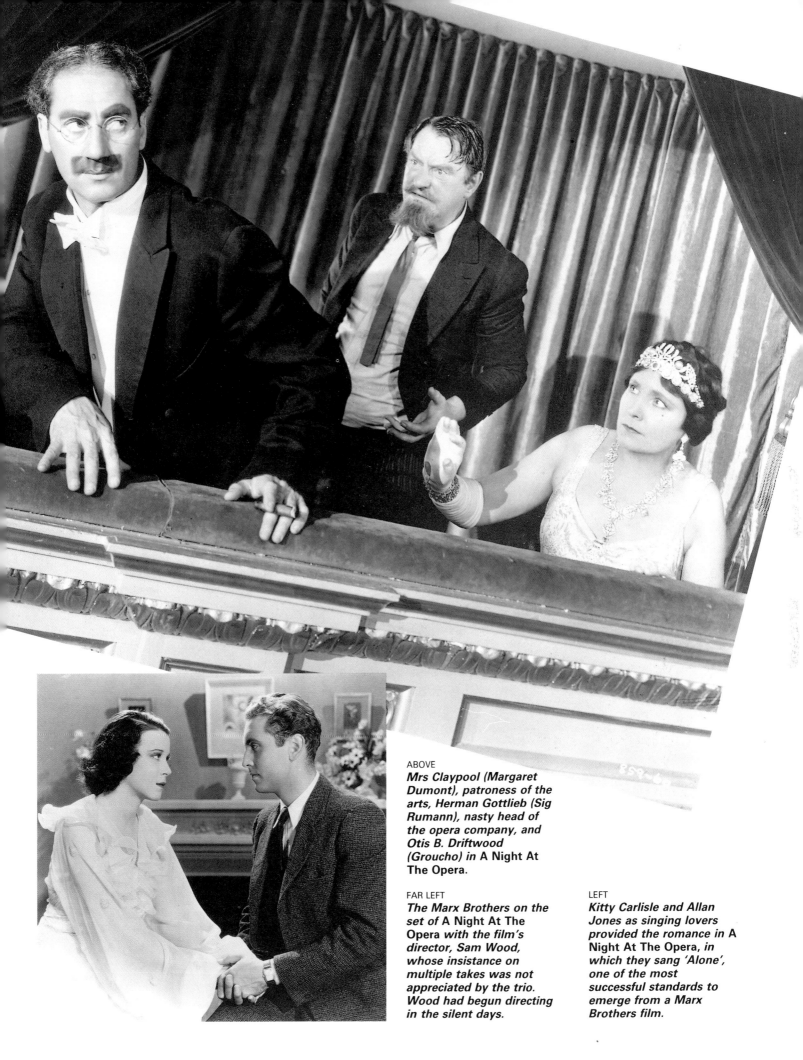

ABOVE
Mrs Claypool (Margaret Dumont), patroness of the arts, Herman Gottlieb (Sig Rumann), nasty head of the opera company, and Otis B. Driftwood (Groucho) in A Night At The Opera.

FAR LEFT
The Marx Brothers on the set of A Night At The Opera **with the film's director, Sam Wood, whose insistance on multiple takes was not appreciated by the trio. Wood had begun directing in the silent days.**

LEFT
Kitty Carlisle and Allan Jones as singing lovers provided the romance in A Night At The Opera, **in which they sang 'Alone', one of the most successful standards to emerge from a Marx Brothers film.**

After further scenes of inspired lunacy, the brothers disrupt a performance of *Il Trovatore* at the Met so that the nasty tenor, who has forced his attentions on the soprano, can be kidnapped and replaced in order to give Baroni his chance. The overture becomes 'Take Me Out to the Ballgame', Harpo and Chico toss a baseball to each other over the heads of the orchestra, and Groucho sells peanuts.

Although glossier, plottier and with longer musical and romantic interludes, *A Night at the Opera* retained many of the best elements from the Paramount films.

"HERE'S TO LOVE"

Dumont: Mr. Driftwood; three months ago you promised to put me into society. In all that time, you've done nothing but draw a very handsome salary.

Groucho: You think that's nothing, huh? How many men do you suppose are drawing a handsome salary nowadays? Why you can count them on the fingers of one hand . . . my good woman!

Dumont: I'm not your good woman!

Groucho: Don't say that, Mrs Claypool. I don't care what your past has been. To me you'll always be my good woman. Because I love you. There. I didn't mean to tell you, but you . . . you dragged it out of me. I love you.

Dumont: It's rather difficult to believe that when I find you dining with another woman.

Groucho: That woman? Do you know why I sat with her?

Dumont: No.

Groucho: Because she reminded me of you.

Dumont: Really?

Groucho: Of course. That's why I'm sitting here with you. Because you remind me of you . . .

Groucho and Chico attempt to agree on a contract in which they get horribly tied up trying to understand 'The party of the first part shall be known in this contract as the party of the first part . . .'

> Groucho: That's what they call a sanity clause.
> Chico: You can't fool me. There ain't no Santy Claus.

There is also an elaborate sequence in Groucho's hotel suite, when Harpo and Chico manage to avoid being caught by a detective by always being one move (or room) ahead of him.

Surprisingly, the movie received few laughs when it was given a sneak preview at Long Beach. Trying to

TOP LEFT
Groucho and Margaret Dumont in A Night at the Opera. Fans consider theirs the greatest love affair in screen history.

LEFT
Harpo and Chico among the chorus of gypsies from Il Trovatore in A Night at the Opera.

ABOVE
What better place was there for the anarchic Marx Brothers to wreak havoc than in the stuffed shirt atmosphere of an opera house in A Night at the Opera. Here, Harpo takes his bow to a trombone in the orchestra pit.

OVERLEAF
**Sam Wood directing the
sequence in A Night at
the Opera, which takes
place in a hotel suite
where the trio has to keep
one step ahead of the
house detective, while
having their breakfast at
the same time.**

BELOW
**Stowaways Chico, Allan
Jones and Harpo,
elaborately disguising
themselves as Russian
aviators in order to avoid
detection in A Night at
the Opera, find they have
to address a mayoral
gathering.**

The New Republic wrote that it was 'one of the most hilarious collections of bad jokes I've laughed myself nearly sick over.'

Many years later the director Mike Nichols met Groucho at a Hollywood party. 'Groucho, I must tell you I've seen *A Night at the Opera* seventeen times.' Groucho was very touched. 'Yes, I just couldn't get over that love story between Allan Jones and Kitty Carlisle!' said Nichols.

After the success of *A Night at the Opera*, Thalberg immediately got the brothers together with Sam Wood again (despite the stars' antipathy towards him), plus screenwriters Robert Pirosh, George Seaton and George Oppenheimer, and Al Boasberg to add gags. After eighteen scripts were written they finally came up with *A Day at the Races*. Oppenheimer, who had written some episodes for the radio show, *Flywheel, Shyster and Flywheel*, claimed that writing for the Marx Brothers

figure out the cause, Chico suddenly thought he had found the solution. 'I know what it is!' he said. 'The mayor of Long Beach died today and everybody was so sad they couldn't laugh.' When it was released in December 1935 it was warmly welcomed by the critics and public alike, earning three million dollars profit. *The New York Times* considered it, 'the loudest and funniest screen comedy of the winter season', while *The New York Evening Post* wrote, 'None of their previous films is as consistently and exhaustingly funny, or as rich in comic invention and satire.' Otis Ferguson in

was not pleasant. 'Groucho would drive me crazy. I like Groucho, but at 7.30 in the morning he might think something was great and later he'd want to change everything. Harpo was sweet. Chico was nothing. He'd only be interested in whether he had as many lines as Groucho.'

As with *A Night at the Opera*, Thalberg followed the pattern of trying the key ingredients out on stage at various theatres. Ideas were tried and thrown away in Minneapolis, Duluth, Chicago, Cleveland, Pittsburgh and San Francisco. Originally, the character of the horse doctor played by Groucho was called Dr Quackenbush, until they were informed by the MGM legal department that there were dozens of real-life Dr Quackenbushes across the country who might sue. 'That's their hard luck,' said Groucho. 'Let them change *their* names if they don't like it. I've already got Quackenbush painted on my shingle.' But for safety's sake, Groucho became Dr Hugo Z. Hackenbush. Unfortunately, a satirical song by Harry Ruby and Bert Kalmar, called 'Dr

Hackenbush', rather in the manner of Groucho's 'Captain Spaulding' from *Animal Crackers*, which went down big on the tour, was cut from the shooting script because of length. However, it was not lost to the world, as Groucho would warble it on every occasion he could – on radio shows, at Army camps during World War II, and for a Decca record in the fifites.

During the first days of shooting, Louis B. Mayer bumped into Groucho at the studio. 'How's the picture coming, Groucho,' he asked. 'What business is it of yours?' replied Groucho. 'We're working for Thalberg.' Three days later, Sam Wood came onto the set with tears in his eyes and announced, 'The little brown fellow has just died.'

Irving Thalberg, only thirty-seven, had died unexpectedly of double pneumonia. He had always been

BELOW

A publicity shot from A Day at the Races *(1937), the second of the Marx Brothers' MGM movies.*

The producer of the film Irving Thalberg, the Marx's guardian angel at the studio, died aged 37.

frail, but was determined to work twelve hours a day. His widow, Norma Shearer, billed by MGM as 'The First Lady of the Screen', only made a few more films and never remarried. The Marxes were devastated at the death of someone whom they felt really understood them. Nevertheless, though it might have been more difficult to be funny in the circumstances, the production of *A Day at the Races* went ahead, and turned out to be an even greater hit than its predecessor.

Margaret Dumont, this time called Mrs Upjohn, hires Groucho to save her sanitarium from bankruptcy, without knowing what his real qualifications are. (Groucho seems to become dean of a college, a lawyer, a hotel manager, and even the leader of a country, without anyone ever checking his references.) One of Groucho's first deeds is to give Dumont a pill the size of a golf ball. 'Are you sure, doctor, you haven't made a mistake?' 'You have nothing to worry about. The last patient I gave one of those won the Kentucky Derby.'

The races come into the plot because the hero (Allan Jones), in love with Mrs Upjohn's daughter (Maureen O'Sullivan), owns a race horse which could help pay off the mortgage on the sanitarium if it wins the big race with Harpo in the saddle. Chico plays Tony, the hustling sanitarium chauffeur who cons Groucho into buying race tips from him while disguised as an ice cream salesman continually crying, 'Getta you ice cream! Tootsie-Frootsie ice cream!'

Besides the eagerly anticipated Dumont–Groucho, Chico–Groucho, Harpo–Authority encounters, and the not so eagerly awaited harp, piano and singing interludes, the film introduced a new element – Harpo urgently trying to communicate something to Chico non-verbally. Which, as the writer Joe Adamson observed, transformed Harpo from a character who *didn't* speak, to one who *couldn't*. With whistles and gesticulations, Harpo finally gets across to Chico, after an attack on the shrubbery, that he is wanted by Hackenbush.

Among the production numbers was a water carnival and Harpo on a trumpet leading a chorus of blacks in the racially stereotypical 'All God's Chillun Got Swing', a sequence now cut from TV showings in the USA. The film concludes with the usual slapstick routine, this time at the races and less effective than in the confines of the opera house.

The critics of 1937 were generally positive, but fans of the Marx Brothers from their earliest pictures began to perceive a softening of their anarchy and a sentimentality creeping in. Most of today's commentators writing about the Marx Brothers consider that the rot began to set in after *A Day at the Races*.

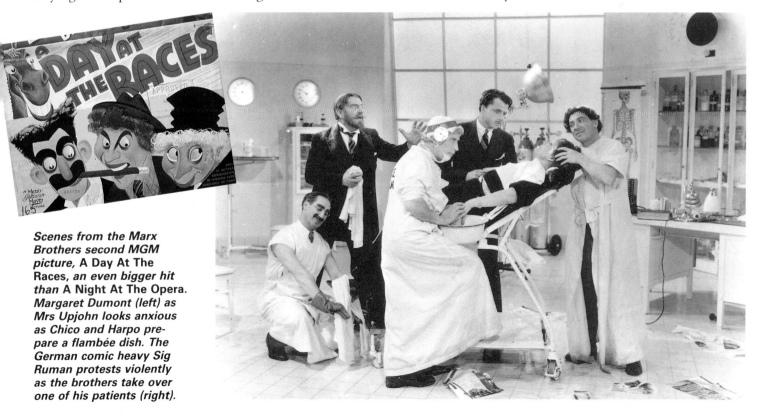

Scenes from the Marx Brothers second MGM picture, A Day At The Races, *an even bigger hit than* A Night At The Opera. *Margaret Dumont (left) as Mrs Upjohn looks anxious as Chico and Harpo prepare a flambée dish. The German comic heavy Sig Ruman protests violently as the brothers take over one of his patients (right).*

6 RUNNING AMOK

In 1938, with the two pictures completed on their MGM contract, Zeppo, acting as his brothers' agent, negotiated a deal with RKO for $250,000. The film was *Room Service*, and this was the first and last transaction Zeppo made for the Marxes. It was also the first and last film of theirs that derived from a source not specifically created for their talents.

RKO had paid a record $225,000 for the film
rights to a play. Written by John Murray and
Allen Boretz, and directed by George Abbot,
it had been a Broadway hit the year before. As
a result, it was one of their least typical movies. 'It was
the first time we tried doing a play we hadn't created
ourselves,' explained Chico. 'And we were no good.
We can't do that. We've got to originate the characters
and situations ourselves. Then we can do them. Then
they're us. If we get a gag that suits our characters we
can work it out and make it ours. But we can't do gags
or play characters that aren't ours. We tried it and we'll
never do it again.'

For Marxian purists *Room Service* was certainly an
aberration, but it is, notwithstanding, quite an amusing
film, with Morrie Ryskind's cleverly adapted screenplay
allowing the brothers some leeway within the confines
of the original play. It concerned a theatrical troupe
trying to avoid being thrown out of a luxury hotel,
while desperately scrounging for money to do a show
and pay their bills. One of their ruses is to pretend that
one of their number has measles and cannot be evicted.
Groucho was the producer of the company, which
included Lucille Ball, Ann Miller and Frank Albertson.
The comic highlights were Harpo downing a gigantic
salad in a few seconds and pursuing a turkey which flies
out of an open window.

The movie (remade as the Frank Sinatra musical, *Step
Lively*, in 1944) was ably directed in five weeks by
William A. Seiter, who had made one of Laurel and
Hardy's funniest features, *Sons of the Desert*. It was
however a box-office disaster, and it lost RKO $340,000.
Fortunately, this did not seem to worry MGM producer
Mervyn LeRoy, who signed the brothers to a three-
picture contract worth $250,000 a movie, with a $50,000
bonus if each film got made for under a million.
Although the death of their father, followed by that of
Thalberg, and the hard work on the road and on the
pictures had made the Marxes feel rather stale, they had

OVERLEAF
Three wise Marxes.
Groucho said of their next
film, 'You know Room
Service *was a funny play.*
RKO . . . had no-one to star
in it. So they came to us
and paid us a lot of money'.

RIGHT
Harpo, Ann Miller, Chico,
Lucille Ball and Groucho
in Room Service *(1938).*
This adaptation from a hit
Broadway farce was the
only one of their films not
specially written for them.

Harpo at home with his harp and wife, actress Susan Fleming, whom he married in 1936.

RIGHT
**Harpo threatening to blow
his brains out in front of
heavy Raymond Burr
(right) in** Love Happy
(1950), **virtually a Marx
Brother movie for Harpo.**

ABOVE
**Groucho makes himself at
home in the courtroom.**

RIGHT
**Groucho in the arms of
Marilyn Monroe in** Love
Happy. **In only her second
credited screen role, the
celebrated sex symbol
made a brief but
memorable appearance.**

mocking himself, not to mention a duel with a Nazi; Chico's piano fingers are as agile as ever, and so is Groucho's deflating wit.

> Groucho:
> (*behind hotel desk*):
>
> Have you got any baggage?
>
> Client: Of course. It's on its way over from the airfield.
>
> Groucho: In all the years I've been in the hotel business, that's the phoniest excuse I've ever heard. I suppose your name is Smith!
>
> Client: No, It's Smythe – spelled with a 'y'.
>
> Groucho: Oh, that's the English version. Mr and Mrs Smythe and no baggage! Let me see your marriage license.
>
> Client: What! How dare you, sir?
>
> Groucho: How do you like that, puts a 'y' in Smith and expects me to let him into the hotel with a strange dame!
>
> Client: Strange dame!
>
> Groucho: She is to me, I've never seen her before.
>
> Client: Sir, you may not be aware of it, but I am President of the Moroccan Laundry Company.
>
> Groucho: You are, well, take this shirt and
> (*undressing*) have it back by Friday! Mr Smythe, or Smith, this is a family hotel and I suggest you take your business elsewhere.
>
> Client: Sir – this lady is my wife. You should be ashamed!
>
> Groucho: If this lady is your wife, *you* should be ashamed.

The distinguished critic James Agee wrote: 'It is unnecessary to urge anyone who has enjoyed them to see *A Night in Casablanca*. It is also beside the main point to add that it isn't one of their best movies for the worst they might ever make would be better worth seeing than most other things I can think of.' However, he hadn't yet seen their following picture, *Love Happy*, released in 1950, the only really bad Marx Brothers movie.

Actually, it could be considered a Marx Brother picture, because the story was conceived by Harpo as a solo vehicle for his marvellous miming. 'Harpo had an idea that he was Charlie Chaplin and wanted to do a film by himself,' recalled Groucho. 'Before you know it they discovered that they couldn't finance the film unless all the Marx Brothers were in it. The banks wouldn't put up the money and that's how I ended up in the film.'

Love Happy not only made the mistake of unbalancing the great three-man act, but it tried to force Harpo into sentimentality. He played a shop-lifting tramp who keeps a troupe of struggling actors from starving as they rehearse a Broadway revue. Dancer Vera-Ellen was the object of his unrequited affections. While Chico popped up occasionally, once on piano in a virtuoso duet with a gypsy violinist, Groucho appeared for no longer than ten precious minutes. 'Some men are following me,' says Marilyn Monroe to private eye Groucho. 'Really, I can't understand why,' he replies. It was only Monroe's second credited screen role, and a very brief one at that.

The whole thing ended with a reasonably imaginative rooftop chase among neon signs. This came about when the financing was running out and the producer Lester Cowan helped raise additional funds by making deals with companies for their names to be advertised on the signs. Later, Groucho sued the producers for $35,000 salary he hadn't received. *Love Happy* was an unhappy experience all round.

It was astonishing, however, that the Marx Brothers had lasted as a popular team in films since 1929. They would appear in the same movie only once more, unwisely placed in different scenes, in the disastrous *The Story of Mankind* (1957). Groucho appeared as Peter Minuit, cigar in mouth, buying Manhattan from the Indians; Harpo was Isaac Newton, who receives hundreds of apples on his head, and Chico played a monk. Also in the cast were Hedy Lamarr (Joan of Arc), Virginia Mayo (Cleopatra), Peter Lorre (Nero) and Dennis Hopper (Napoleon). The brothers were seen together for the very last time in 1959 on TV in *The Incredible Jewel Robber*, a wordless and mirthless thirty

minutes with an ailing Chico, an aged Harpo, and Groucho making a short entrance at the end. There were other plans to bring them together again, but their ways in show business had parted permanently.

Groucho continued his career independently, but the bright spark of his talent was only permitted to flicker in the ghastly films he was in. In *Copacabana* (1947), wearing his own moustache, hair and clothes, he ran

TOP LEFT
The Three Marx Brothers fooling around for the benefit of the cameras on the sound stage of United Artists' Love Happy, *not the happiest of their pictures.*

ABOVE
Vincent Price, appropriately playing the Devil, with Ronald Colman, cast as the Spirit of Man, on the set of The Story of Mankind.

LEFT
Chico, ridiculously cast as a Spanish monk in The Story of Mankind *(1957), listens patiently to the dreams of Anthony Dexter as Christopher Columbus.*

TOP RIGHT
Groucho, as an agent, opposite 'Brazilian Bombshell' Carman Miranda in Copacabana *(1947). This cheaply-made musical was a low point in both their careers.*

around frantically as Carmen Miranda's agent. In *Mr Music* (1950), he sang, danced and clowned with Bing Crosby in a feeble number called 'Life Is So Peculiar'. In *Double Dynamite* (1951), he played a waiter who is an expert on crime, and spends a great deal of the time leering at Jane Russell whose attributes were suggested by the film's title. In *A Girl in Every Port* (1952), he was a wised-up sailor in partnership with his dim-witted mate, William Bendix and, finally, in *Skidoo* (1968), he portrayed a racketeer known as 'God' in a cast that included a number of other has-beens – Jackie Gleason, Peter Lawford, George Raft, Cesar Romero and Mickey Rooney.

Among his TV performances was the role of Ko Ko in Gilbert and Sullivan's *The Mikado* broadcast in April 1960, which also included his fifteen-year-old daughter Melinda as one of the 'Three Little Maids From School'.

But for fourteen years from 1947, Groucho had been in the American public's eye, first on radio and then TV, as the acerbic host of the quiz show, *You Bet Your Life*. He was astonished by its success. 'This certainly proves I know nothing about show business. We get a sponsor [the Elgin-American Watch Case Company], not because he thinks the show is any good, or because he thinks I'm a great comedian, but because he thinks it's the cheapest show he can buy. And what happens? It sweeps the country and I turn out to be a bigger name than I ever was on Broadway.'

Aside from his radio, TV and film appearances, Groucho did a lot of writing. Way back in 1937 he had co-written (with Norman Krasna) the screenplay for a Warner Bros. comedy starring Joan Blondell called *The King and the Chorus Girl*, and (also with Krasna) a 1948 Broadway play, *Time For Elizabeth*. (Groucho played

the lead in a TV revival in 1963). In addition, he wrote his sketchy but funny autobiography, *Groucho and Me* (1973). He published his selected letters a year later, including his correspondence with American poet T. S. Eliot.

Chico's only solo appearances, besides those in nightclubs, was in a road company production of *The Fifth Season*, but an angina condition prevented him from working. Financial woes continued to plague him, and

TOP LEFT
Groucho comforts Jane Russell in Double Dynamite **(1951). The title was changed from** It's Only Money **to stress Russell's most famous attributes.**

BOTTOM LEFT
Frank Sinatra, Jane Russell with Groucho in Howard Hughes' Double Dynamite.

BELOW
Groucho continued to work for many years in different fields; acting, writing, compèring and singing, as seen here recording an album in the sixties.

121

his brothers kept coming to the rescue. On 11 October, 1961, the oldest of the Marx Brothers died in his sleep at the age of seventy-four in the modest bungalow he and his second wife, Mary, rented in Beverly Hills. Arthur Marx wrote that Groucho had always predicted that Chico's life would probably come to an end in bed 'but out of shotgun wounds, not angina pectoris; and not in his own bed, but in some other husband's.'

At the funeral, Harpo turned to Groucho and asked how he was feeling. 'Better than Chico,' he replied. 'Wanna make a bet on which one of us goes next?' asked Harpo. 'I'll give you three to one, and take either corner.' It was Harpo, who also suffered heart trouble. He died soon after undergoing open-heart surgery on 28 September, 1964 at the age of seventy-five. 'He inherited all my mother's good qualities – kindness, understanding, and friendliness. I got what was left,' said Groucho.

ABOVE
Guest star Harpo making a rare television appearance in the fifties with another great clown, Lucille Ball, in an episode in the popular I Love Lucy *series.*

RIGHT
All five of 'Minnie's Boys' photographed together again in the late fifties: (from left to right) Harpo, Zeppo, Chico, Groucho and Gummo.

BELOW
Sixty-four-year-old Groucho Marx with his twenty-one-year-old third wife Eden Hartford in 1954. The marriage lasted fifteen years.

RIGHT
Groucho arm in arm with Erin Fleming, the Canadian would-be actress who became the comedian's 'companion' in the last years of his life.

Arthur Marx (left), Groucho's son, who was involved in a long and sordid legal battle with Erin Fleming (right) over who was to be the old *man's conservator. It lasted until Groucho's death on 19 August 1977, a sad end to a wonderful career in show business.*

Certainly, Groucho, in his old age, lived up to his adopted name. His second marriage to Kay lasted three years, because all 'she wanted to do was stay home and wash her hair'. In 1954, the sixty-four-year-old Groucho announced he was to marry a twenty-one-year-old former model, Eden Hartford. Surprisingly the marriage lasted fifteen years, although they were an ill-matched pair. He criticised her for being uneducated, yet when she tried to better herself by learning French, taking up the piano and attending acting classes, he undermined her confidence, and she gradually turned to alcohol. In 1971, at the age of eighty-one, Groucho met Erin Fleming, a twenty-nine-year-old Canadian would-be actress, who became his 'companion'. She also became very protective of him, and handled most of his business affairs. As he grew more and more frail in mind and body, so Erin took over more and more,

prompting a sordid legal battle between her and Groucho's son, Arthur, over who was to be the old man's conservator. The wrangle lasted until the star's death on 19 August, 1977. Gummo had died earlier in the year, and Zeppo followed in 1979.

The Marx Brothers were gone, but they are still very much alive through their films which are shown to the delight of generation after generation. During the Vietnam war, *Duck Soup* was shown around the colleges, and became a cult. Barbra Streisand dresses as Harpo in the fancy dress party scene in *The Way We Were* (1977);

and the brothers have been the subject of two Broadway musicals, *Minnie's Boys* (1970) starring Shelley Winters, and *A Day in Hollywood, a Night in the Ukraine* (1982), written by Frank Lazarus and Dick Vosburgh. The series *Flywheel, Shyster and Flywheel* was revived successfully on BBC radio in 1990 featuring the remarkable mimicry of Michael Roberts and Frank Lazarus.

Duck Soup is, of course, the movie Woody Allen chooses to go and see in *Hannah and her Sisters* to cheer himself up after he has been diagnosed (incorrectly) as having cancer. He comes out of the film feeling better about life – an emotion shared by audiences for over half a century and proof that the Marx Brothers' brand of comedy has never dated.

FILMOGRAPHY

The director is indicated in brackets.

Paramount Studios

1929
The Cocoanuts (Joseph Santley and Robert Florey)
Groucho, Harpo, Chico and Zeppo

1930
Animal Crackers (Victor Heerman)
Groucho, Harpo, Chico and Zeppo

1931
Monkey Business (Norman McLeod)
Grouch, Harpo, Chico and Zeppo

1932
Horsefeathers (Norman McLeod)
Groucho, Harpo, Chico and Zeppo

1933
Duck Soup (Leo McCarey)
Groucho, Harpo, Chico and Zeppo

Metro-Goldwyn-Mayer

1935
A Night at the Opera (Sam Wood)
Groucho, Harpo and Chico

1937
A Day at the Races (Sam Wood)
Groucho, Harpo and Chico

RKO Radio Pictures Ltd

1938
Room Service (George Abbot)
Groucho, Harpo and Chico)

Metro-Goldwyn-Mayer

1939
At the Circus (Edward Buzzell)
Groucho, Harpo and Chico

1940
Go West (Edward Buzzell)
Groucho, Harpo and Chico

1941
The Big Store (Charles Riesner)
Groucho, Harpo and Chico

United Artists

1943
Stage Door Canteen (Frank Borzage)
Harpo

1946
A Night in Casablanca (Archie Mayo)
Groucho, Harpo and Chico

1947
Copacabana (Alfred E. Green)
Groucho

1950
Love Happy (David Miller)
Groucho, Harpo and Chico

Warner Bros

1957
The Story of Mankind (Irwin Allen)
Groucho, Harpo and Chico

Paramount

1950
Mr Music (Richard Haydn)
Groucho

1963
Skidoo (Otto Preminger)
Groucho)

RKO

1951
Double Dynamite (Irving Cummings)
Groucho

1952
A Girl in Every Port (Chester Erskine)
Groucho

Twentieth Century-Fox

1957
Will Success Spoil Rock Hunter? (Frank Tashlin)
Groucho in cameo role

TV

1947–1961
You Bet Your Life
Groucho

1960
The Mikado
Groucho and his daughter Miriam

INDEX